I0814114

Melbourne Hall Garden

Melbourne Hall Garden

Jodie Jones
Photography by Andrea Jones

Contents

Title page The essential elements of the magnificent garden at Melbourne Hall have remained extraordinarily unchanged over the course of three centuries.

Opposite Streams of clear water have always flowed through the gardens, but in recent years their ornamental aspect has been gloriously heightened by the artistic planting schemes created by Marie-Claire.

Foreword
Robin Lane Fox

Like all good gardens, Melbourne Hall has evolved. Its evolution has been exceptionally long with more than three hundred years behind it. It is a fascinating story and as this invaluable book shows it is not finished yet. It sweeps us through Melbourne's earlier history more clearly and accessibly than ever before and includes many twists and turns that will intrigue admirers of historic English gardens and prove to be authoritative for garden historians. The chapters on the garden's design and planting since 1987 are a rich source for contemporary designers and planters whatever the scale of their projects. They are rooted in years of practical experience, distilled here for the first time.

Melbourne Hall survives as a grand garden with a plan from the early eighteenth century, even though it opens off a populous town in Derbyshire, and it has two principal characters. One is Thomas Coke, eventually Vice Chamberlain at the court of Queen Anne, and the other is Marie-Claire, who has brought an artistic eye to the garden's replanning and planting during the past thirty-seven years. Each of them embarked on grand gardening when only twenty-five.

I am intrigued by this book's new account of Thomas Coke. Melbourne usually features in handbooks on garden history because of its wrought-iron Birdcage, designed quite brilliantly by Robert Bakewell from 1704 onwards. There was much more to Coke's garden art. Receipts for some of his plants show that he was a major participant in the passion for ornamental gardening that had been flowering in early modern England long before parks and grassy landscapes of the Georgian age became Europe's idea of the 'English garden'. I can well relate to his lists 'of Things had of ye seedsmen' and 'Mixt Tulip Roots', and to his topiary evergreens and 'tubyroses'. He was not a narrow-minded exponent of nothing but native plants. His eye had been widened by travels in Europe, especially to grand gardens in France. The pre-eminent nurserymen, George London and Henry Wise, interacted importantly with him, but I prefer this book's suggestion that he himself was the garden's mastermind. Under William and Mary and Anne, other talented landscapers were prominent at court. During Coke's work at Melbourne, Robert Benson, Anne's Chancellor of the Exchequer, was laying out a superb landscape garden at Bramham Park in Yorkshire, shaped by formal French taste but also best attributed to his own design.

Coke emerges as 'a courtier, sociable man-about-town and a fond father'. In this generation Ralph and Marie-Claire also rank as sociable and are fond parents of six children, but as an artist Marie-Claire brings a painterly eye to bear too. Her work at Melbourne is an important example of gardening informed by a painter's art, a tradition in England that includes John Piper and Cedric Morris. She is admirably clear that a bigger picture must precede details fitted into a garden, just as it does in a good painting. The chapter on her choices of trees is a tribute to her venturing with expert help off usual tracks. Her rare oaks and limes are maturing proofs of her careful positioning, even in groups of three and five. Her sense of colour is truly painterly, whether in her blend of fritillaries, scillas, purple-black tulips and white camassias in green grass, or pink and rose primulas beside water with a controlled blend of lemon, lilac and lime shades nearby. Against brick walls she is now busy contrasting pale-flowered roses and genuine red ones according to the times of day they are struck by sunlight.

She neatly compares her life of gardening to her life's work in raising six children. This book takes us beautifully through the family trails that underlie Melbourne and its garden, which has been extended by her routine of vigilance and love.

Robin Lane Fox, Autumn 2024.

Opposite Shafting sunlight heightens the impact of the ancient Yew Tunnel, planted 300 years ago to clothe a neat timber trellis, but now gnarled into characterful old age.

Map

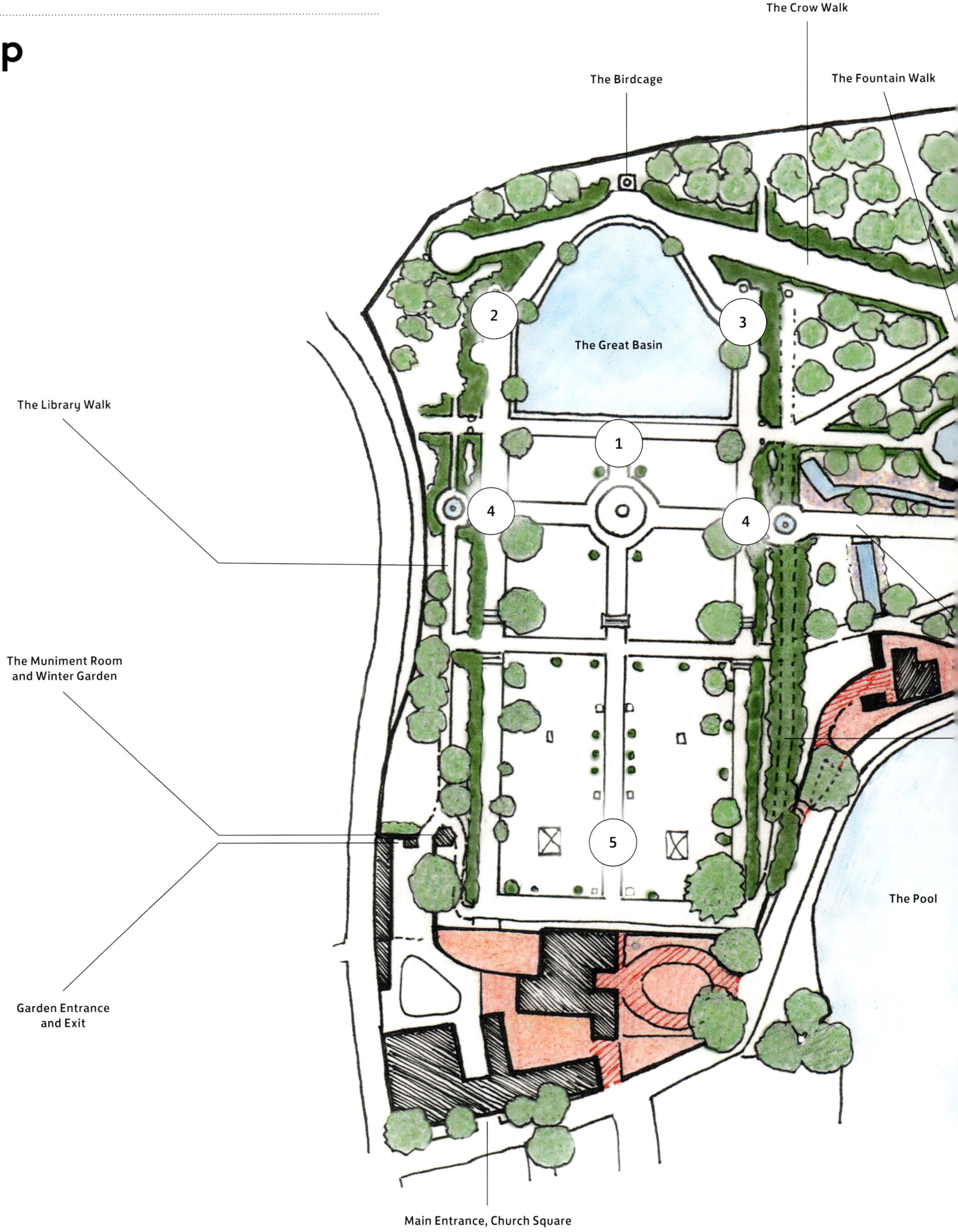

The Crow Walk

The Birdcage

The Fountain Walk

1

2

3

4

4

5

The Great Basin

The Library Walk

The Muniment Room
and Winter Garden

Garden Entrance
and Exit

The Pool

Main Entrance, Church Square

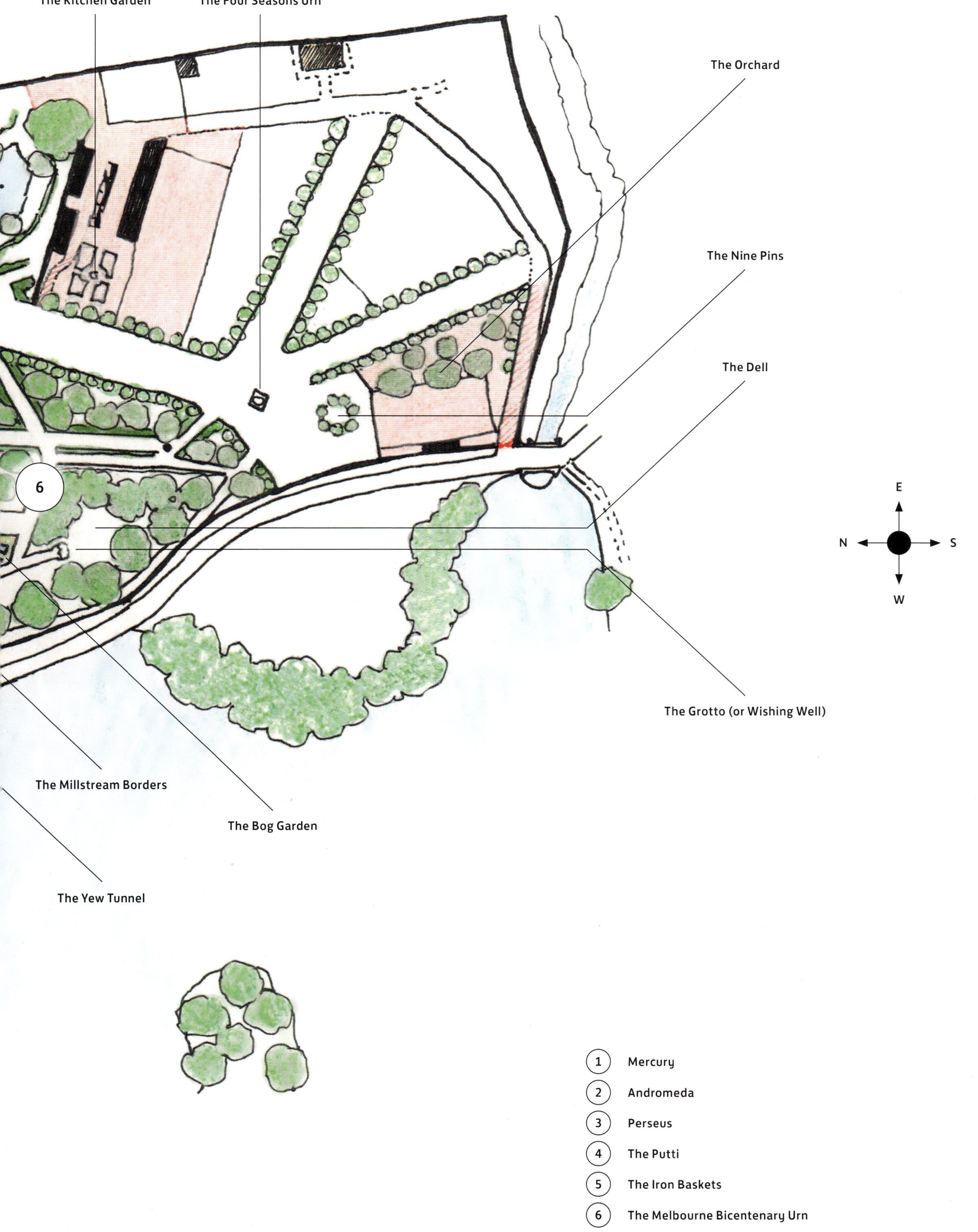

1 Mercury
2 Andromeda
3 Perseus
4 The Putti
5 The Iron Baskets
6 The Melbourne Bicentenary Urn

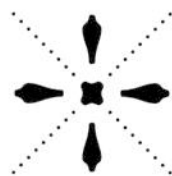

Introduction

Opposite This is a garden of vistas, many of them unchanged with the passing of centuries, and Thomas Coke would instantly recognize this view from the Coaching Ring, across the sloping lawns and down to the Great Basin.

Step out into the gardens of Melbourne Hall in the silent light of an early morning, and you leave the twenty-first century behind. Before you spreads a swoop of green lawns and a grid of gravel pathways framed by enormously undulating yew hedges, leading to the still expanse of the Great Basin, where a soft mist invariably hovers over the mirror-like surface of the water. It is a view that has scarcely changed since the Rt. Hon. Thomas Coke drew up his masterplan for the grounds over 300 years ago, and today it draws thousands of garden visitors and garden historians from all over the world to this quiet corner of Derbyshire.

The gardens at Melbourne Hall are widely agreed to be the finest surviving English example of the early-eighteenth-century Anglo-French formal style, popularized by King Louis XIV's overtly awe-inspiring gardens at Versailles. That they are drawn on a relatively domestic scale makes the intelligence of their design and the charm in their details even more apparent. There are fountains still powered by the original system, cast-lead statues that have scarcely moved since they were first installed and a magnificent wrought-iron structure, known as the Birdcage, which has been continually celebrated since it was first unveiled in the early 1700s. In total, more than twenty different original features within the garden hold a Grade 1 listing, all remarkably untouched by the passage of time even as their setting has gently evolved and matured.

Unlike so many stately home gardens, which are now managed by bureaucratic trusts, Melbourne Hall continues to be a family home today, as it has been through a large part of its history, ensuring a personal investment in the place that has kept its spirit alive as well as its fabric maintained. It is currently occupied by Ralph, the Marquis of Lothian, a direct descendent of Sir John Coke, the Secretary of State to Charles I who purchased the estate lease in 1629 and whose great grandson, the Rt. Hon. Thomas Coke, laid out the gardens in the formal design that we still appreciate today. Since 1987 Melbourne Hall has also been home to Ralph's wife Marie-Claire, the Marchioness of Lothian, a professional artist and inspired horticulturist. She has not only raised their family here but has also made many sensitive additions to the gardens, which respect their historic importance while breathing new life and colour into their botanical composition.

Fortunately, the story of how this extraordinary garden was created has been preserved in vivid detail in the estate archives. These contain many boxes filled with personal correspondence, letters of professional engagement and statements of account that vividly illustrate just how heavily Thomas invested his time and energy, as well as his finances, in the creation of his gardens. Those many age-softened sheets of paper, with their faded ink and cracked seals of thick red wax, serve as a window on the past, providing us with a rare ringside seat at the unfolding of events.

The garden was not, as is sometimes mistakenly reported, designed by London & Wise, the leading garden makers and nurserymen at the turn of the eighteenth century, although they did supply Thomas with vast quantities of plants and consulted with him on the relative merits of his own creative ideas. There are letters in the archive from both George London and Henry Wise, but there is also a great volume of correspondence chronicling the daily detail of the project written by Thomas's unmarried sister Elizabeth, generally known as Betsy. She oversaw work on the gardens when Thomas's duties as Vice Chamberlain to Queen Anne kept him away from home, and her witty observations and entertaining turns of phrase bring this whole lengthy and laborious process gloriously to life.

The gardens were a life's work for Thomas, who kept adding refinements right up until his death in 1727 but, for the next hundred years or so, the Hall became a secondary seat of the family and was little visited. After a brief renaissance as a family seat in the 1820s to 1840s, Melbourne Hall was occupied by a series of Victorian tenants who conscientiously discharged their duty to maintain the property but showed little inclination to develop the grounds and had even less incentive to do so. It is entirely thanks to this period of benign indifference that Thomas's garden escaped the fate suffered by so many other fine formal gardens of the early eighteenth century, which were erased less than fifty years after they had been completed by the 'improving' habits of Capability Brown and his acolytes. At great expense, they swept away stone terraces, broad gravel paths and fine yew topiaries, then replaced them with faux natural lakes, wooded copses and grazing pastures that they laid right up to the doors of many a stately home around the country. Melbourne Hall, with its backdrop of gently rolling hills and expansive neighbouring lake, known as the Pool, could easily have been made to fit the Capability Brown template. Instead, it remained a sleeping beauty, safe within its perimeter of mellow stone and brick walls.

In due course, the property passed via the female line to Lord Melbourne, the first of Queen Victoria's nine prime ministers and the man who gave his name to Australia's second largest city. He made some additions and improvements to Melbourne Hall, but it was never his primary residence, and it was not until the Kerr family permanently returned to Melbourne Hall in 1905 that the maintenance of the garden became a particular focus of attention. More recently, when Ralph and Marie-Claire made it their family home, the garden was once again in the daily care of a passionate and creative gardener.

Right The classic view of Melbourne Hall, with the spire of Melbourne parish church rising over its roofline, is beautifully reflected in the surface of the Great Basin.

Opposite top An impressive Atlas cedar (*Cedrus atlantica*) stands sentinel on the main terrace, framing a view across the formal gardens and out into the parkland beyond the boundary.

Opposite bottom left A portrait of Ralph, painted in oils by his wife Marie-Claire.

Opposite bottom right Marie-Claire with a trug full of tulips, freshly picked to decorate the house.

Above Marie-Claire has an artist's eye for plant combinations, drawing together specimen trees, such as the layered wedding cake tree (*Cornus controversa* 'Variegata') and coral bark maple (*Acer palmatum* 'Sango-kaku'), with a rich palette of herbaceous plants.

Right Although the gardens are on a grand scale, individual groups of plants can be surprisingly dainty and finely considered, as in this pretty combination of lavender asters, pale pink Japanese anemones and purple *Verbena bonariensis*.

Marie-Claire Black had grown up surrounded by beautiful gardens in Cornwall and Scotland, then spent several years in Spain as apprentice to the artist Joaquim Torrents Llado, and she first came to Melbourne Hall to paint a portrait of the young Ralph. This proved to be the most important commission of her life, since it led to love, marriage, and the discovery of an extraordinary ability to garden creatively and to paint with plants.

Marie-Claire began by gently releasing the outer reaches of the garden from encroaching Victorian shrubs, and planting new colour-themed borders in the spaces this created. In due course she also restored the yew hedges that flank the glorious wrought-iron Birdcage, which is such an important focal point for the formal heart of the gardens. Then, while raising her six children and continuing to paint the portraits of many notable society figures, she continued with a series of interventions and additions to the gardens, driven by a desire to make them as botanically stimulating as they were historically interesting.

The full story of this exceptional location has never been told until now, when it can be illustrated by the beautiful work of photographer Andrea Jones, who has chronicled the progress of the gardens through the seasons and over the course of many years. The result is an archive of images that complete the portrait of a remarkable garden created by two extraordinary individuals, divided by the passage of 300 years but united by a common love for this very special place.

Below Much of the garden is boldly architectural in both content and effect. Here, the grass edge of the Great Basin, a bulging horseshoe of yew hedge, and the aged trunk of a swamp cypress (*Taxodium distichum*), frame the famous gilded Birdcage.

Overleaf At its heart, the garden at Melbourne Hall is a perfectly preserved example of early eighteenth-century formal design, surrounded by a beguiling 'wilderness' which has matured over the centuries.

SIR JOHN COKE.
CORNELIS JANSSENS 1590 1664.

Chapter 1
In the Beginning

Opposite A fine portrait of Sir John Coke still hangs in Melbourne Hall, the Derbyshire property he acquired in 1629.

In 1629 Sir John Coke was looking for a place in the country. He was Secretary of State to King Charles I, and a significant figure in royal circles who had also held high office in the courts of Queen Elizabeth I and King James I. Like every other nobleman keen to reinforce his position, it was important that he was a frequent presence in court circles, and he maintained a fine residence at Garlick Hill, in the heart of the city of London but, like well-heeled Londoners ever since, he also wanted a fine country residence to reinforce his status and provide a place where he could retreat and regroup from time to time.

The capital at that time had a population of around 300,000 and was a place of some prosperity and excitement, but life there was not without its perils, even for the monied upper classes. The air was often thick with a foul-smelling smog caused by the burning of sea coal. Bubonic plague was still endemic, and in fact an outbreak had killed an estimated 40,000 Londoners just four years previously. Fire was also a permanent danger in a city filled with houses made from wood (a threat that was to be most dreadfully realized in 1666, when the Great Fire killed an estimated one quarter of the city's population).

Political turbulence meant that court life was challenging as well. King Charles I had just declared the dissolution of Parliament that was to last for eleven years, presaging the political turbulence of a reign that would end, extraordinarily, with his beheading on 30 January 1649.

All in all, although he already owned a house in Herefordshire, it isn't surprising that 66-year-old Sir John decided he would like to acquire another bolthole in the countryside. Having been born in Derbyshire, he chose to take on the estate at Melbourne with a view to retiring there in due course.

If refuge was his motivation for choosing Melbourne, then he was unconsciously echoing the very origins of his new property, which had been established almost 500 years earlier, in 1133, when King Henry I appointed Adelulf, Prior of Nostell in Yorkshire, as the first Bishop of Carlisle.

In the twelfth century, the borderlands between England and Scotland were a wild and frequently warlike place, and King Henry consequently gave his new bishop a parcel of land in Melbourne as a safe haven where he could retreat whenever the skirmishes threatened to rampage out of control. The Domesday Book records show that there was already a church and incumbent priest on the site in 1086, but it is thought that the present-day Melbourne parish church, which is unusually magnificent for such a small town, was built either by Adelulf or by the king himself on a scale suitable for it to serve as an

TO THE GLORY OF GOD

Opposite The parish church of St Michael with St Mary's has stood alongside Melbourne Hall for hundreds of years, although the poignant War Memorial in Church Square is a more recent addition.

intermittent cathedral. Whatever the truth of its origins, successive Bishops of Carlisle continued to use Melbourne as a retreat throughout the thirteenth and fourteenth centuries. Certainly, there must have been a house on the site of Melbourne Hall by the early thirteenth century, because at that time Bishop Walter Mauclerc was an occasional resident and was able to obtain a royal grant for an annual fair and a weekly market in the town.

By the early fifteenth century, the area around Carlisle had become relatively peaceful, and its bishops no longer felt the need for a Derbyshire bolthole, so they began leasing their Melbourne estate to laymen. The earliest known tenant was Thomas Cromwell, notorious Chief Minister to King Henry VIII, who in 1530 agreed to pay £10 a year in rent. He was followed by a number of other notable gentlemen, none of whom appear to have used it as their primary residence, or to have taken much notice of a clause in their leases that required them to maintain the house at Melbourne 'with thacking [thatching] and daubing in all things necessary'.

Consequently, when, in 1595, Sir Francis Needham of London signed up as the latest tenant of the Melbourne estate, he found that the house and outbuildings had fallen into 'exceeding greate decaye, especially the mansion house which is utterly ruined and inhabitable without greate and chardgable reparacions'. Unlike some previous lessees, Sir Francis actually wished to live there and his solution, implemented over the next two years, was to pull down and rebuild a large part of the house; the oldest surviving masonry in the present-day house is thought to date from this period.

We know from various plans and documents that the house as Sir Francis remodelled it had a layout very similar to that of the Hall today, with a large forecourt to the south where the carriage circle now draws up to the front door, and the main family rooms situated in the east wing looking out over the gardens. However, the external appearance of the house would have been very different, with leaded windows, tall chimneystacks and an origami arrangement of interconnecting pitched roofs.

That may conjure a picture that appears rather magical from a twenty-first century perspective, but it would probably have looked decidedly dated to contemporary eyes at the time when Sir John Coke took over the estate, under a combination of leasehold and freehold agreements, in 1629. Almost immediately, Sir John decided that drastic action was necessary to make the building suitable for his occupation. Maybe the complicated roofscape was no longer proving to be entirely waterproof, because an old-fashioned appearance alone was unlikely to have held huge sway over a man known to his contemporaries as 'the last Elizabethan' – a nickname he had acquired partly in recognition of his faithful service to Queen Elizabeth I right up until her death in 1603, but primarily because he was widely reputed to be one of the most conservative men in the country.

Whatever his reasons, within a few months of acquiring the deeds Sir John had begun planning substantial alterations to his new property and, in order to keep proper track of the works, he instructed that the house and grounds be surveyed and mapped. The resultant plan still exists in the estate archives, the ink faded but clearly legible on a large sheet of creamy velum, which has been neatly folded in half at some point in the intervening centuries. It shows elements that are recognizable today, including the hexagonal Muniment Room (which was then a dovecot) and a mid-fifteenth century timber-framed barn, which now forms part of the Craft Centre, although the gardens then were significantly smaller and bounded on all sides by public roads.

At that time a busy main highway ran between Melbourne Hall and the church, past the Pool to a watermill, fields, common land and then onwards towards Ashby-de-la-Zouch. Meanwhile, on the east side of the house a lane separated the grounds of Melbourne Hall from Blackwall Hall, which was then another significant house although it was demolished soon after, in the 1640s (although it is still commemorated today in the name of Blackwell Lane).

As the plan of 1629 clearly shows, Sir John's garden was relatively small, ending roughly in the middle of the upper parterres of the present-day gardens. Nevertheless, it included a banked-up terrace along the east front of the house with hedges, a bowling alley and grass plats (or lawns) in a formal, symmetrical

arrangement. On a lower level, there were also stew ponds (where fish were kept in a sort of living larder to supply the table), a kitchen garden and an orchard – all practical staples of any gentleman's estate at that time. A heavy stone wall cut across the entire garden, surprisingly close to the house, roughly in a line from the Muniment Room, and further walls completed the boundary, protecting the garden from undesirable elements outside.

We have no detailed description of Sir John's garden but can deduce from contemporary accounts of other gardens that it would have been a charming and intimate space. The walls were most probably lined with espaliered fruit trees and the beds would have been filled in season with violets and primroses, peonies and lily of the valley, lavender, roses and lilies. Since the well-to-do at that time regarded their orchards as something of a status symbol, Sir John is also likely to have grown figs, apricots, cherries and grapes as well as a good number of different apples and plums, and the kitchen garden would have contained various herbs, salad leaves, radishes and sorrel, alongside the staple beans, peas, beets, leeks and parsnips.

Opposite Historically, trained fruit, such as this fastigiate pear tree, would have been picked, carefully packed and sent on to the family wherever they were residing at the time.

Below The eighteenth-century fruit walls have over the centuries, supported an extensive range of glass houses (indicated by the sections of white-painted wall).

The productive garden was important for supplying the practical needs of the household, but the ornamental garden was at that time increasingly seen as a social space – a private extension away from a house full of servants. Many contained a gallery structure along one or several of the walls that provided shelter from the elements and allowed the household to walk through the grounds untroubled by sun or rain. We don't know for sure if there was such a gallery at Melbourne, but it would have been a natural precursor to the Yew Tunnel that is such a prominent feature today. In addition, the most fashionable gardens would also have contained a fountain in a stone basin, set into the centre of the quartered lawns, but this may well have been a flourish too far for the conservative Sir John.

It is clear that he put significant time and trouble into improving his country estate, but his role in the court of Charles I would have left him with little free time to spend in Derbyshire, and there is evidence that he may not actually have felt this to be much of a loss. When his son, Sir John Coke the Younger (1607–50) announced his own intention of moving to Melbourne, Sir John Sr. wrote a bluntly worded letter of warning. 'You shal plant yourself in a town where there are manie beggars, most pore & but a few good livers.' On top of which, local folk would 'ingage you into debates and suites wherin little is to bee gotten but vexation & troble to no end'.

Left Mown paths cut a romantic swathe through the long grass, ox-eye daisies and buttercups of the old orchard.

In fact, it was actually some of the local 'good livers', in particular Sir John Harpur of nearby Calke, who ended up causing the Cokes their greatest difficulties. Harpur appears to have become outraged when, in 1638, Sir John Coke Sr. and Sir John Coke the Younger unilaterally enclosed an area of common land between Melbourne and Calke known as Derby Hills.

The Cokes were far from the only landowners at that time to indulge in the practice of appropriating common land. Across the country it has been estimated that some 40,500 hectares (100,000 acres) were enclosed in the two decades leading up to the 1650s. But by enclosing Derby Hills, the Cokes fell foul of the local commoners who understandably resented the loss of their traditional rights of access to the land. The wrath of Sir John Harpur, in contrast, might perhaps be attributed more to irritation that he had been outmanoeuvred and therefore missed out on bagging a valuable parcel of land for himself. Either way, the Cokes' actions made them extremely unpopular in the area.

Revenge being a dish best eaten cold, it was not until two years later that a mob of Royalist soldiers on their way north appear to have been encouraged by a quantity of free ale and a £10 bribe to destroy the new fences and set fire to a water mill recently built by the Cokes. According to a contemporary report, the people of Calke and a neighbouring village 'hooted and capered and rejoiced exceedingly at the mischief', and the rampaging soldiers threatened that if the fences were repaired before their return, they would 'pull Sir John Coke out of his house', 'pull the house down about his eares' and set fire to Melbourne village.

The fact that all associated parties were staunch Royalists, at a time when Oliver Cromwell and the Parliamentarians were increasingly expressing their dissatisfaction with the rule of King Charles I, appears to have made no impact on local hostilities between the landowners.

Their squabbles were, however, forgotten when Civil War did finally break out in 1642. The elder Sir John Coke immediately fled from the advancing Parliamentarian army. His son chose to stay on in Melbourne and seems to have felt sufficiently secure in his position to expend considerable energy pursuing a long-held wish to enlarge his gardens by absorbing into them a public road that then bounded the east side of the estate. In 1647 he had made a contract with the seventy-six householders then living in Melbourne by which they individually signed away their rights to the road in question, Dove House Lane. In recompense, Sir John agreed to maintain an adjacent road, now called Blackwell Lane, at his own expense in perpetuity.

Right Green shaded tunnel walks were once common in all the great gardens. The Yew Tunnel at Melbourne Hall is an original feature that has acquired great character along with great age.

Right A portrait by Sir Peter Lely of Colonel John Coke and his wife (née Lady Mary Leventhorpe), the parents of Thomas Coke, still hangs in the dining room.

Opposite The view from the library windows out to the Carriage Circle, framed by heavy curtains and a pleasing jumble of books and music, has changed little over the centuries.

As a side note, in 1926 the local Trent Buses company wanted to use Blackwell Lane for a new route, but determined that the road was not being maintained to a high enough standard for their vehicles to drive down it. At that time, the owners of the Melbourne Hall estate, the Kerr family (who had inherited, via several twists and turns down the female line, from the Cokes), were still paying for the maintenance of the lane, but the original seventeenth-century agreement had been long lost and forgotten and they believed themselves to be the legal owners. After a certain amount of wrangling with the bus company, the family eventually received £200 compensation to sign away their 'ownership' of the route. The true facts only came to light in 1985, when estate archivist Philip Heath discovered the original 1647 document while listing the large collection of estate deeds. (To this date, the family has not been asked for a refund!)

As it turned out, Sir John Coke the Younger got little opportunity to enjoy his newly expanded gardens. By 1648, with the outbreak of the Second English Civil War raising alarm bells, he finally decided it would be expedient to seek refuge in France. He died there just two years later without ever coming back to England.

During the Commonwealth period that followed the execution of Charles I in 1649, Melbourne was neglected and the church was wilfully damaged by some elements within Oliver Cromwell's army. By the time the monarchy was restored with the coronation of King Charles II in 1660, the Melbourne estates were in a poor condition and had passed to the third generation of the family in the person of a seven-year-old boy, also called John and later to be known as Colonel Coke (1653–92).

At the age of twenty Colonel Coke married Mary Leventhorpe, a wealthy heiress from Hertfordshire, and set about using her money to turn the house and gardens into a suitably splendid family home. A double portrait of the couple, painted by Sir Peter Lely, still hangs on the wall of the dining room. In the picture, Mary is holding a red carnation and the pair are depicted against the backdrop of an expansive landscape, looking every inch the proud owners of a significantly improved property.

It appears to have been the colonel who oversaw several modifications to the gardens, including an extension of the terraced section near the house, which he achieved using the land made available when Sir John the Younger acquired the old Dove House Lane. The redesigned garden reached down to the brook at the bottom of the valley that still flows through the garden today.

Colonel and Mary Coke went on to have seven children in just eight years, and five of their offspring are shown standing alongside their parents in a 1680 painting by Jacob Huysmans that still hangs in the house. The group includes five-year-old Thomas Coke (1675–1727), a cherubic looking little boy in ringlets and lace who was next in the family line to inherit Melbourne Hall and would go on to devote his life to creating the gardens that survive and thrive to this day.

Right No one knows exactly when the matched pairs of the Indian bean tree were planted up the main lawns, but this native of the eastern United States was originally introduced to Britain in 1726.

Francis Bacon on Early Seventeenth-Century Gardens

Opposite Rather like Thomas Coke, Sir Francis Bacon was an English courtier and statesman, appointed by King James I as Lord Chancellor of England, but also a passionate lifelong gardener who wrote a seminal essay on their proper design.

In 1625, Sir Francis Bacon wrote an essay entitled *Of Gardens*, which conveys a good sense of the prevailing views of the time and, directly or indirectly, may well have informed Sir John Coke's aspirations for his garden. It certainly gives modern readers and garden visitors some sense of what the grounds of Melbourne Hall would have been like in the early seventeenth century.

Bacon was a philosopher, scientist, and prolific commentator who had been Lord Chancellor of England (the highest legal post in the kingdom) until 1621, when he was charged with accepting bribes and was forced to retire. Perhaps he had that recent disgrace in mind when he wrote 'God Almighty first planted a Garden and, indeed, it is the purest of human pleasures; it is the greatest refreshment to the spirits of man; without which, buildings or palaces are but gross handy-works.'

Unfortunately for most modern-day readers, his assessment of the acceptable scale for a significant garden decreed that 'the contents ought not well to be under thirty acres of ground'. He was keen on lawns that, he said, offered two pleasures: 'the one, because nothing is more pleasant to the eye than green grass kept finely shorn; the other, because it will give you a fair alley in the midst, by which you may go in front upon a stately hedge, which is to enclose the garden.'

He very sensibly recommended that gardens should contain something of interest in every month of the year, while admitting that from late November until the end of January this would mainly be provided by evergreens including holly, ivy, juniper and fir trees. However, his list also included orange trees, lemon trees and myrtles 'if they be stoved' (i.e. moved out of the winter cold and kept in a hothouse), making it clear, if there were any doubt, that this was gardening advice for the one per cent.

Bacon made particular mention of the importance of scent, including the violet, which 'above all others, yields the sweetest smell in the air', musk roses and 'Wallflowers, which are very delightful to be set under a Parlour or lower chamber window', although he also extolled the fragrance of 'Strawberry leaves dying, with a most excellent cordial smell', which is less easy to relate to.

He thought that the heart of a garden should be square and enclosed on all sides with 'a stately arched hedge' trained on pillars of carpenter's work. On either side of this he envisioned a 'diversity of side alleys' for further strolling, accessed by a 'covert alley' created 'upon carpenter's work, about twelve foot in height, by which you may go in shade into the Garden'.

Overcoming the elements and avoiding the heat of the summer sun were a primary consideration at a time when only manual labourers would have allowed the sun to colour their complexions. He also highlighted the importance of alleys that 'must be ever finely gravelled, and no grass, because of going wet.'

He thought fountains were 'a great beauty and refreshment' but said 'Pools mar all, and make the Garden unwholesome and full of flies and frogs'.

Flanking the formal elements, he advocated a 'Heath', or wilder part of the garden, like the ornamental meadows that are currently all the rage:

> *For as for shade, I would have you rest upon the alleys of the side grounds, there to walk, if you be disposed, in the heat of the year or day, but to make account, that the main garden is for the more temperate parts of the year, and in the heat of summer, for the morning and the evening, or overcast days.*

TERTIUS
A PLATONE
PHILOSOPHIÆ
PRINCEPS
III
IV
V
VI

Chapter 2
Thomas Coke: The Man and His World

Opposite Thomas Coke (1675–1727), painted in his youth by Swedish portraitist Michael Dahl, whose work was very highly regarded by British aristocrats and the royal family.

The Rt. Hon. Thomas Coke was born in 1675, fifteen years after King Charles II had been restored to the British throne. After a period of enormous political disturbance national life was finally settling down, and it is likely that the young Thomas enjoyed an idyllic early childhood in Melbourne.

The garden that he grew up in was, like all large gardens of that age, laid out in a very orderly fashion. At a time when the natural world still held plenty of dangers and inconveniences, a predominantly rectilinear design was a reassuring sign that man-made civilization ruled the world inside its secure boundary of walls and hedges. The garden at Melbourne Hall provided the whole Coke family with a safe space for outdoor pursuits well away from the inconveniences of rutted roads and muddy fields, and for the seven children, above all, it must have been an excellent place to play.

In due course, like most well-bred young men of his day, Thomas was sent away from home for schooling. Later he attended the University of Oxford, spent some time being tutored in the Netherlands and, it is thought, studied architecture and garden design in France as well. All in all, by the time he inherited Melbourne Hall in 1696, this well-travelled and well-read young man was fully aware of all the latest trends and ready to make his mark, both at home and on the wider political stage. To this end, he set about securing either a seat in parliament or a place within the royal court hierarchy, despite the intermittent periods of turbulence that still occasionally disturbed life in the country.

A letter from his sister Alice, sent to him at Melbourne towards the end of 1696, gives a dramatic snapshot of life in London in the months following a plot to assassinate King William III which had been foiled in February of that year:

> *Dear Brother, You are happy that you are quietly taking recreation in the country, and only hear at a distance of tumults and bustles that are every minute in the town. Sometimes there's a report sent abroad that a hundred and twenty blunderbusses are ready charged to kill his Majesty, wherever he goes, but his good angel defended him from them all. Immediately upon this all the gates of the City are shut, and all that can't give an account of themselves are clapped up till they can, and then set at liberty again . . . Sometimes for three or four days there's mighty searching of houses for people that they say are lately come out of France: and some say they have found several of them, and some say they can't find, and others that there's none to find. Thus everybody says a different thing, and nobody knows anything, but the want of money; and everybody agrees in that complaint. I was at London yesterday, and am so tired with hearing of nothing but*

disorders and tumults and hurrying into prison and letting out again that I almost made a resolution to go no more this winter.

Thomas certainly enjoyed the tranquil retreat that Melbourne offered him, and in 1698 began the lavish spending on his garden that was to continue for the rest of his life. However, he was also keen to get out and distinguish himself, and in that same year successfully stood for election as the Member of Parliament for Derbyshire. When his great friend and contemporary Robert Jennens wrote to congratulate him on winning at the tender age of twenty-three, he attributed this triumph to Thomas's cosmopolitan credentials. He would, said Jennens, be 'as proper a man to serve the nation in the House of Commons as any that will be there; for by your travelling and conversation in the world I believe you know the circumstances of Europe as it now stands as well as anybody.'

Both Thomas and Robert travelled widely in their youth, as was the custom for young men of their social standing at that time. In fact, Thomas seems to have been a positive gadabout for a while. The estate archives are filled with notes from various members of his family wondering when he was planning to finally come back home. In 1696 his brother, John Coke wrote to him in Antwerp to say: 'I hope by this time you have almost wearied yourself with rambling, and begin to think of home. If you abscond much longer I will go into the country to take possession.'

His sister Alice was also regularly in touch, but she expressed herself in rather more sprightly terms:

Dear Brother, We had not the satisfaction of hearing of you till last Tuesday. I have heard a thousand things since you went concerning your journey. Some fancy it was no further than a private lodging in town upon some secret design . . . Others again say that your seeing the country is to spend this part of the summer with some of the sisters of your society in Suffolk . . . Whenever I am asked, I say, as you told me, that you are soberly going to see the north part of England, and intend to be back again in September.

Robert Jennens also roamed widely, and his letters to Thomas give some sense of what life was like for these young court acolytes. At one point Robert accompanied King William III to Loo, in the Netherlands, where they pursued an exhausting programme of hunting, particularly of stags. There was, however, sport of a different kind as well. Writing on 17 October 1698, Robert recounts in great detail the quality of the hunting and the standard of their various mounts, but also notes, 'On Saturday came the Electress of Hanover, and brought with her several of the Hanover ladies; one or two very handsome, but the rest generally of the largest size.'

In fact, thanks to Robert we know that Thomas was by no means just a sober-living courtier and gardener. The two young men clearly enjoyed what might euphemistically be called an active social life, despite the fact that Thomas married Mary, daughter of the Earl of Chesterfield in 1697, when he was twenty-two years old, and she had given birth to their first child, a daughter called Mary, at the beginning of 1700.

Writing in August 1700 Robert, himself newly engaged, chastises his friend for giving him advice on married life:

I am favoured with my dear Coke's letter of the 6th, but he writes so very wickedly to a man that's resolved to be wondrous good, that he must excuse me if I condemn his ways, and advise him to reformation. Since matrimony has been so far from mending you, that it has made you rather worse, lest it should have that ill effect on me, that am in a kind of state of righteousness, I could almost resolve to change my design, was not inclination and honour very prevalent.

For Thomas, one consequence of his married state was simply that there was yet another person writing to ask when he might be planning to come home. As a new mother, Lady Mary Coke spent a lot of her time at Melbourne, and sent more than a few letters asking her husband to join her there. When he lost his parliamentary seat at the start of 1700, she wrote to him in London to say:

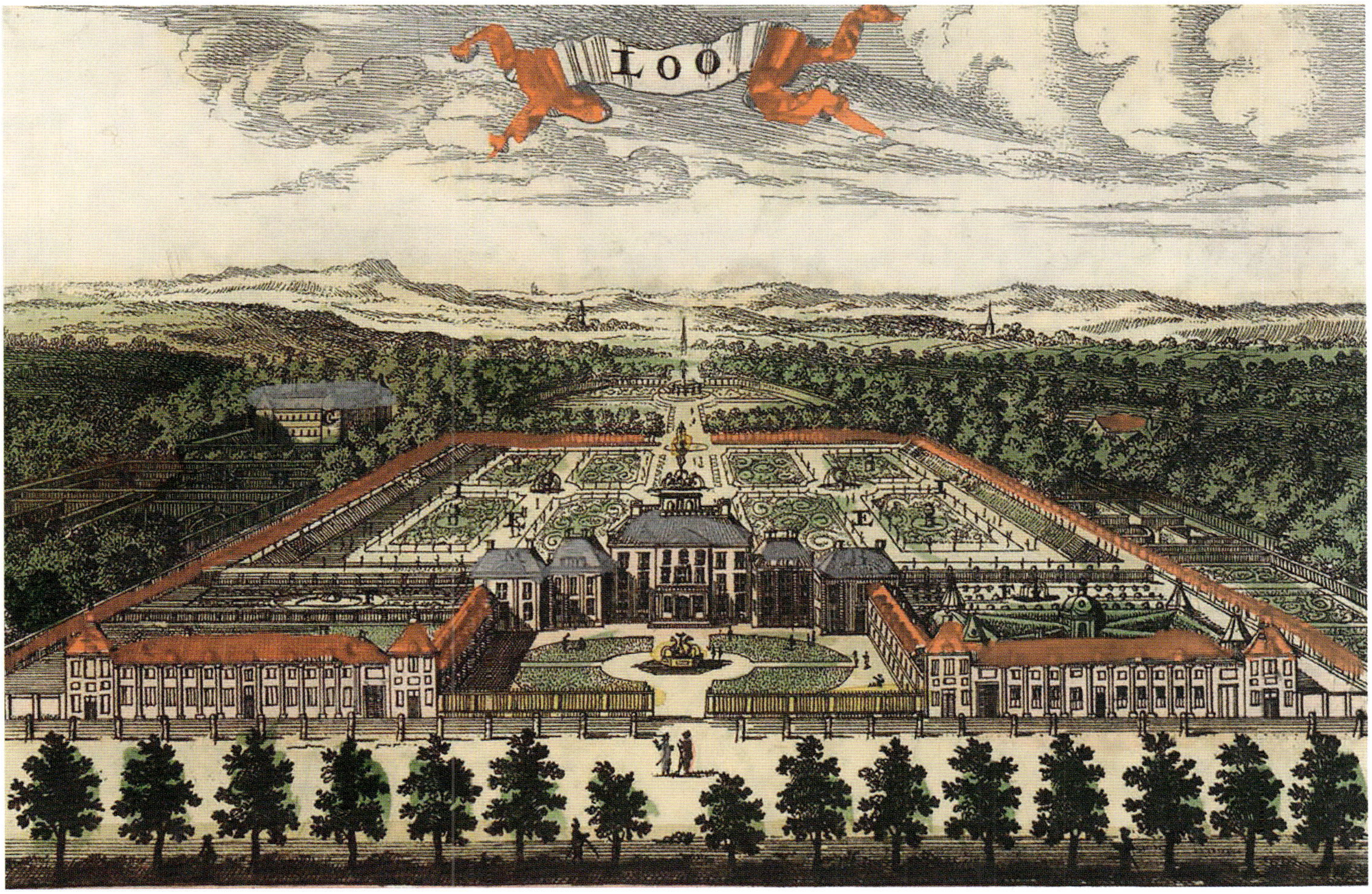

Above The Palace of Het Loo, in the Netherlands, with its magnificent formal gardens, was home to William and Mary until they jointly acceded to the English throne in 1689, and they took it as their inspiration when remodelling the gardens at Hampton Court Palace.

Left *William III Hunting at Het Loo* (*c.*1696) by Dutch artist Dirk Maas (1659–1717).

ELIZABETH COKE

Opposite Thomas Coke's sister Elizabeth, known to her family as Betsy, was a prolific and highly entertaining correspondent, whose eyes twinkle with mischief and merriment even in the formal portrait which still hangs in Melbourne Hall.

Though I ought to be a little sorry, my dear may have been a little disappointed in the affairs of the election, yet give me leave now to rejoice that I may hope to have you soon with me, which is the real pleasure of my life; and also that I may reasonably expect to have more of your company than if you had been a Parliament man.

In fact, despite having lost his position as a Member of Parliament, Thomas soon found himself called back to London on terms described by his father-in-law, the Earl of Chesterfield to Lady Mary:

Since I writ to you last, dear daughter . . . Mr Coke came just now to me, and told me that he has sent for you to town, because the House of Commons have made him one of the six commissioners for stating the accounts of the nation. This employment will be extremely laborious, continues but for one year, and the salary is but £500 a year, which is no great matter for so continual an attendance: but I hope this will be an introduction to something that will be much better.

This is equivalent to around £83,000 at today's prices, which few outside the earl's rarefied social circle would have described as 'no great matter'. Even Thomas might have found the salary coming in handy as his family soon increased in size. Lady Mary gave birth to their second child, another daughter, who they named Elizabeth, in their London home at St James's Place in 1703.

There was the usual relief and congratulation for mother and baby having survived the very real perils of childbirth in that time, although this was tinged with a note of commiseration that no son and heir had yet been produced. This was most amusingly articulated by Lord Stanhope, Lady Mary's brother, who wrote to Thomas Coke in April, 'to wish you much joy of your daughter . . . I believe I might have had a nephew had it not been prevented by the pernicious influence of too many cucumbers.'

In any case, the relief and congratulation turned out to be premature. Shortly after being brought to bed, Lady Mary was writing to her husband from the spa town of Bath to complain that 'these two days past I have had two violent fits of the cholic, indeed as severe as any at London.' Any question that she might have been complaining unnecessarily is answered by a paper in the archives dated 17 January 1704 listing 'particulars . . . for the funeral of Lady Mary Coke'. These included 'two Pennons wrought on crimson silk, £5-0s-0d', and '12 Shields at 3s per piece'.

Five days later her heartbroken father, the Earl of Chesterfield, wrote to Thomas:

Since I find that I have not strength enough of mind (on this occasion) to come to you as I ought, permit me to make use of this means to express the high sense I have of all the kindness that you showed to my poor daughter; and to assure you that though she is gone, I shall always embrace your interest as my own, and value the two poor infants that she has left as a tie of our inviolable friendship . . . But these thoughts do so tear my soul that I must crave some time to be allowed me before I can speak calmly after such a storm, that has disordered my remaining life, and made me lose all the comfort and joy that remained to an old man, who is your most affectionate father and very unfortunate servant.

Even 300 years later, his distress is so heartfelt and so clearly conveyed that it positively tears at the heartstrings. Thomas, meanwhile, seems to have grieved in a different way. He continued to spend most of his time in London or accompanying the royal court on its travels, although always consumed with thoughts of his Derbyshire garden. There is a letter in the archive dated 6 January 1705 in which Walter Burdett of nearby Foremark writes to Thomas that 'I despair of your coming into this country til your garden invites you'. Thomas's passion for Melbourne Hall was widely recognized by his contemporaries, but we know far less about the corporeal loves in his life.

For a woman to die following childbirth was not uncommon at that time, and there is no surviving record to indicate how hard Thomas was hit by the loss of his wife, but there does appear to have been a certain amount of speculation amongst his contemporaries about how long it would take him to replace her, and he doesn't seem to have liked it.

Left The snow may come and go, and the glazed billiard room was added relatively recently in the early twentieth century by Lord Walter Kerr, but the main approach to Melbourne Hall has remained otherwise unchanged for hundreds of years.

A draft of a letter sent in August 1704 by Thomas to someone called Keightly still radiates with his outraged disapproval:

> *At my coming into Derbyshire I was surprised with an account of some things you said here in town to a sempstress whose sister lives at Kedlaston, which is so silly a lie that till I hear how you can clear yourself, I have too good an opinion of you to believe. What I am told you said was that Sir Nathaniel Curzon's daughters were gone to the Bath to try to get them husbands, but you believed to no purpose; and that Sir Nathaniel Curzon had offered either of them to me with £20,000, and that I had refused them. This last it lies more immediately upon me to expect you to clear yourself [from]: and the rest I hope you can for your own sake; for I have that kindness for you that I should be sorry to have any occasion to write myself other than your affectionate friend.*

Whether anyone offered him £20,000 or not, Thomas did not rush to remarry, although as a young and well-to-do widower he would surely have been regarded as fine husband material. In May 1706 a W. Stratford of Christ Church, Oxford, wrote to him implying as much:

> *You may now have leisure to finish your fine gardens, and when they are done you may sit in security under your own vines and fig trees . . . I suppose this fine seat is designed only to please yourself, for as to any design you may have on any lady there can be need of nothing but your own person and address.*

The Melbourne gardens may have been a solace to Thomas but his father-in-law, the Earl of Chesterfield, whose elaborate gardens at nearby Bretby were widely reputed to be second only to those at Versailles, was still so shaken by the loss of his daughter that it seems he could find little pleasure in any aspect of his life. Writing a few weeks after W. Stratford, he told Thomas that:

> *. . . now my daughter is gone from me I am become a perfect hermit, for nobody can live a more solitary life. And since you are pleased to mention my gardens, I will tell you that I was never less pleased with them, for my orange trees are almost spoiled, as having neither fruit nor blossoms, nor hardly any leaves: and the ponds of water I made for my waterworks have lost all their water. These things might be counted disaster to a person who is in the affairs and bustle of the world. But in my opinion there is so little of that which men call happiness to be found anywhere, that all conditions are almost alike, and I am sure must have the same ending.*

Right Just before sunrise, the Birdcage stands silhouetted against a hazy backdrop of parkland, while the water of the Great Basin is invariably wreathed in mist.

Opposite The serene portrait of Thomas Coke's young daughters Mary and Elizabeth, which today hangs in the billiard room, gives no hint of the endless trouble their fidgety hijinks caused the artist, Michael Dahl.

Thomas's little girls must have been equally heartbroken by the loss of their mother, although their Aunt Betsy, Thomas's unmarried sister, took on a maternal role in the early years. In amongst all the lively news and gossip included in her letters to Thomas, Betsy always took care to ask his opinion and permission for every decision relating to their care, and his considered responses would seem to mark him out as a fond, albeit often physically distant, father.

Court business had always kept him in London for much of the time, but this pressure increased further when, in 1706, he was appointed a Vice Chamberlain of the Household, which required him to be almost constantly waiting in attendance on Queen Anne. Fortunately, Betsy was on hand to keep him involved in all the minutiae of his daughters' affairs, from the purchase of a new coat when an old one had been outgrown, to timing their weaning from milk to solid food.

These day-to-day events were recounted by Betsy in a steady stream of correspondence which, even from a distance of three centuries, is still highly entertaining. As well as local gossip and tales of her own exhaustingly active social life, the exploits of the two little Coke girls provided Betsy with a rich source of material. Mary, the older of the two girls, seems to have been a particularly spirited child who kept the entire household on their toes and gave her aunt plenty to worry about.

In October 1706, Betsy wrote to Thomas with an anxious account regarding a bout of ill health that appeared 'to be occasioned by [Mary's friend] Miss Katie Bertie and her both eating paper, and also acorns; which I much fear may occasion her ill health some time hence; as well as the eating green apples last year did, with the same little ringleader to mischief.' On another occasion, Betsy was dragged out of church by the alarmed servants when Mary was discovered to have broken her arm, although no one ever worked out how it had happened, and the patient certainly wasn't willing to explain.

The magic of Betsy's writing is that it brings to vivid life a cast of characters long gone who might otherwise appear rather two dimensional. Take the portrait of Thomas's daughters by Michael Dahl, which still hangs in the hall. To modern eyes it appears rigidly formal, as do the children it depicts. In contrast, the letters that Betsy wrote about the process of its painting will resonate with anyone who has ever tried to get a small child to sit still for any length of time: 'Mary has sat the first time for her picture with a great deal of good humour, but so very much motion, that it put Mr Dahl upon great difficulty to catch her in the posture he desired.'

A month later Betsy reported on a second attempt which was every bit as fraught as the first:

> *I can give you but a very ill account of our proceeding as to her picture, for there was no persuasions nor contrivance that we could think of could prevail with her to be half a moment at a time in a posture. Mr Dahl tried an hour at a time twice, but the second time he said he found it impossible to do it to his satisfaction, and therefore desired it might be deferred till her coming to town again.*

In October 1709, doubtless conscious of the need to produce a male heir, Thomas did finally take a new wife, confusingly also called Mary (the Hon. Mary Hale) and once again Betsy was quick to ink her pen and let her brother know what she was thinking:

> *I am satisfied I need not make use of much expression in what you're so well assured as my best wishes to you and yours, particularly in what is so material to your chief happiness in this life . . . Your daughters both desire their humble duty may be accepted by yourself and their new mother, who they have great joy in the thoughts of, and are very full of great resolutions how good they will be, and I may answer for them as far as their years will allow.*

We know little about this second marriage, except that it did produce the longed-for son, George, in 1715, and another daughter, Charlotte, in 1719. Thomas continued in the role of Vice Chamberlain until his death in 1727 but the work that really inspired him, and has proved to be his lasting legacy, was the creation of his beloved garden.

Left The rich autumn colour of a towering swamp cypress (*Taxodium distichum*) provides a striking contrast to the deep green undulations of the yew hedge which frames Robert Bakewell's celebrated Birdcage.

Above Melbourne Hall has always had an extensive productive garden, although these days its harvest includes cut flowers for the house as well as fruit and vegetables for the kitchen.

Right Thomas Coke grew a huge number of tender fruit trees, trained against south-facing walls specifically built for the job. Today that tradition continues, which means that sun-warmed peaches are there for the picking in their season.

Opposite In addition to the walled kitchen garden, there is a separate orchard in the outer reaches of the garden which, in recent years, has been softened with wildflowers and meadow grasses.

The Kitchen Garden and Glass Houses

Until very recently, the primary function of any garden, including those attached to great houses, was to supply the household with kitchen produce. This fundamental dependence on the land only really dwindled in the twentieth century and, even then, a large portion of the head gardener's time would have been devoted to the efficient production of food.

At Melbourne Hall the tradition continues today, albeit on a more modest scale, in a pretty kitchen garden that is bordered by walls that the Rt. Hon. Thomas Coke built at the beginning of the eighteenth century. This is the working heart of the garden, housing the gardeners' mess room where piles of seed catalogues sit next to the teabags and biscuits, and a cavalcade of wheelbarrows is lined up against the potting shed wall. Some years ago Marie-Claire turned her considerable energies to redesigning and improving this area as well.

An enormous and obsolete greenhouse was dismantled and the ground where it once stood was transformed into an attractive potager, with a formal layout of four large beds divided by grass paths and arranged around a central *Crataegus orientalis*. A plaque on the wall carries a touching inscription, dedicating this combination of the practical and pretty sides of horticulture, to Ken Hicklin, who gardened at Melbourne Hall for almost his entire life and, as Head Gardener, was Marie-Claire's cherished ally through her early days here.

Today, depending on the season, the potager beds might be filled with squash or globe artichokes, mixed salads, peas and runner beans clambering up twisted hazel supports. Mixed in with the produce, rows of tulips are followed by sweet peas, zinnias, cosmos and dahlias, providing Marie-Claire with rich pickings for the beautiful flower arrangements that she loves to create for the house.

There are also two rows of cold frames filled with even more flowers for cutting. The selection changes every year, but you will usually find interesting sunflowers and gladioli alongside the tomatoes and herbs. A fruit cage with a wall-trained 'Peregrine' peach tree produces baskets full of delicious sun-ripened fruit, there are generous supplies of rhubarb and raspberries and, in the south-easterly corner of the wider garden, a productive orchard filled with a selection of old apples and a few pears keeps the family supplied with top fruit for much of the year.

In recent years, Marie-Claire has allowed the grass to grow long in the orchard, encouraging the emergence of various wildflowers, including ox-eye daisies and buttercups, which now support a wide range of insects and invertebrates as a rich source of pollen. Mown paths encourage human visitors to explore and add an important element of intentionality to this delightfully informal space.

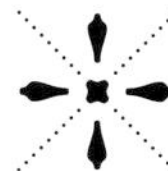

Chapter 3
Garden Design in Thomas Coke's Day

Opposite *Promenade of Louis XIV along the Northern Flowerbed in the Gardens of Versailles* (detail) by Etienne Allegrain (1644–1736).

At the time when Thomas Coke was developing plans for his gardens in the seventeenth century, all the most fashionable horticultural trends were emanating from the continent, in particular from France, where the designer André Le Nôtre was creating gardens of an intentionally awe-inspiring size and scale for the Sun King, Louis XIV.

In the relatively flat land around Paris, Le Nôtre expanded the gardens at the Palace of Versailles to an unprecedented extent, with formal, geometric arrangements of intersecting avenues and paths running for miles out across the surrounding countryside. It was an astonishingly expensive exercise, but Louis enthusiastically embraced this opportunity to demonstrate his mastery over his people and his country.

Work began at Versailles in 1661, involved literally thousands of labourers, and went on for nearly forty years. In the end, the gardens Le Nôtre laid out covered nearly 810 hectares (2,000 acres). There were parterres, groves of trees, pools, hundreds of statues and miles of formal trees and hedges. The already impressive ground plan was further enhanced by optical illusions including the false perspective of tapering avenues, which were cunningly designed to make them appear even longer. In addition, there were elaborate fountains so complex that they could not be operated all at once. Instead, the gardeners would scurry ahead of the king as he strolled, switching each fountain on just before he arrived to enjoy the display and, equally importantly for the preservation of water pressure in a gravity-fed system, switching each one off again as soon as he had passed by.

It was the most celebrated garden of the age, created on a scale that even other monarchs were unable to match. They could and did, however, set out to emulate many of the underlying design principles. Foremost among these was the imposing geometrical arrangement of axes leading off from a central line that ran straight out from the centre of the house facade, preferably towards some distant, eye-catching feature on the horizon. Onto this strict grid were added additional cross axes which ran off out of sight into the green depths of wilder groves and orchards.

The English royals were enthusiastic adopters of this continental style. Queen Henrietta Maria, the French-born mother of Charles II, had already brought celebrated French designer André Mollet over to work on her gardens at Wimbledon House some time before the Civil War. Her son Charles, having spent the years following his father's execution in exile in France, was equally deeply steeped in these great continental influences by the time the crown was restored to him in 1660.

Right Inspiration for well-heeled garden owners was available through books filled with engraved illustrations, such as this design of four square parterres and a circular fountain, created by André Mollet.

Opposite top As a young man, Thomas Coke visited the royal gardens at the Palace of Versailles, south-west of Paris, where the celebrated designer André Le Nôtre worked on an astonishing scale.

Opposite bottom This 1736 engraving of St James's Palace, with the Privy Garden designed by André Mollet visible in the centre distance, would have been familiar to courtier Thomas Coke.

Within a few months of returning to England Charles started work on restoring the royal gardens, which had suffered badly during the years of Oliver Cromwell's Protectorate. Charles was keen to transform his recovered estates with the help of the celebrated Le Nôtre but, knowing him to be the favourite designer of the French king, he first wrote to ask Louis for permission to proceed. Louis replied to the effect that he had constant need of Le Nôtre but would not prevent him accepting a commission if Charles was really determined to appoint him. As it turns out, however, that seems to be exactly what Louis did, since there is no record of Le Nôtre ever having travelled to England. He did send some plans, around 1662, which formed the basis of the design for the royal park at Greenwich, but otherwise Charles's aspirations were thwarted.

Charles instead followed his mother's lead and engaged her favoured designer, André Mollet, to improve his properties. Mollet may not have had the Sun King's stamp of approval, but he came from a famous family of gardeners and had plenty of experience of working on a grand scale to inject a fashionable continental fizz into the gardens of the English great and good. Charles set him to work on the garden of St James's Palace and at Hampton Court, where he is thought to have been involved with creating the impressive canal that today is known as the Long Water, flanked by imposing double avenues of lime trees.

In his book *Le Jardin de Plaisir* (1651), Mollet declared that a 'Garden of Pleasure' should include 'ground works, Wildernesses, choice trees, Palissades and Alleys or Walks, as also in Fountains, Grotto's and Statues, perspectives, and other such like Ornaments.' From a present-day perspective, the gardens he created may appear to have exemplified a pared-back formal aesthetic based on extensive networks of gravel paths and grassy parterres, but in fact his plans typically also included the sort of ornamental woodlands known as *bosquets* in France, as well as palisades of evergreens trained up wooden trellis structures to form shaded walkways, and ornamental flower beds filled with seasonal bulbs, flowers and decorative shrubs.

Inevitably, where the king led his people followed and Thomas, as a loyal courtier, would have had first-hand experience of all these fashionable improvements. His long personal connection to the royal court is underlined by a letter written to him by his friend Robert Jennens in October 1699. 'Yesterday I was at Hampton Court. The King's apartment is finished, and I fancy 'twill be made the prettiest place in the world. The King [William III] will give us all country apartments: we shall be much there, for he likes the place extremely.'

Around the country, the landed nobility rushed to follow the royal example, and there was an explosion of garden improvements on the grandest of scales. Few of these remodelled

St James's Palace and Parts adjacent.

Right The magnificent extent of the Hampton Court Palace gardens at the time when Thomas Coke knew them is celebrated in this astonishing bird's-eye view painted by Leonard Knyff.

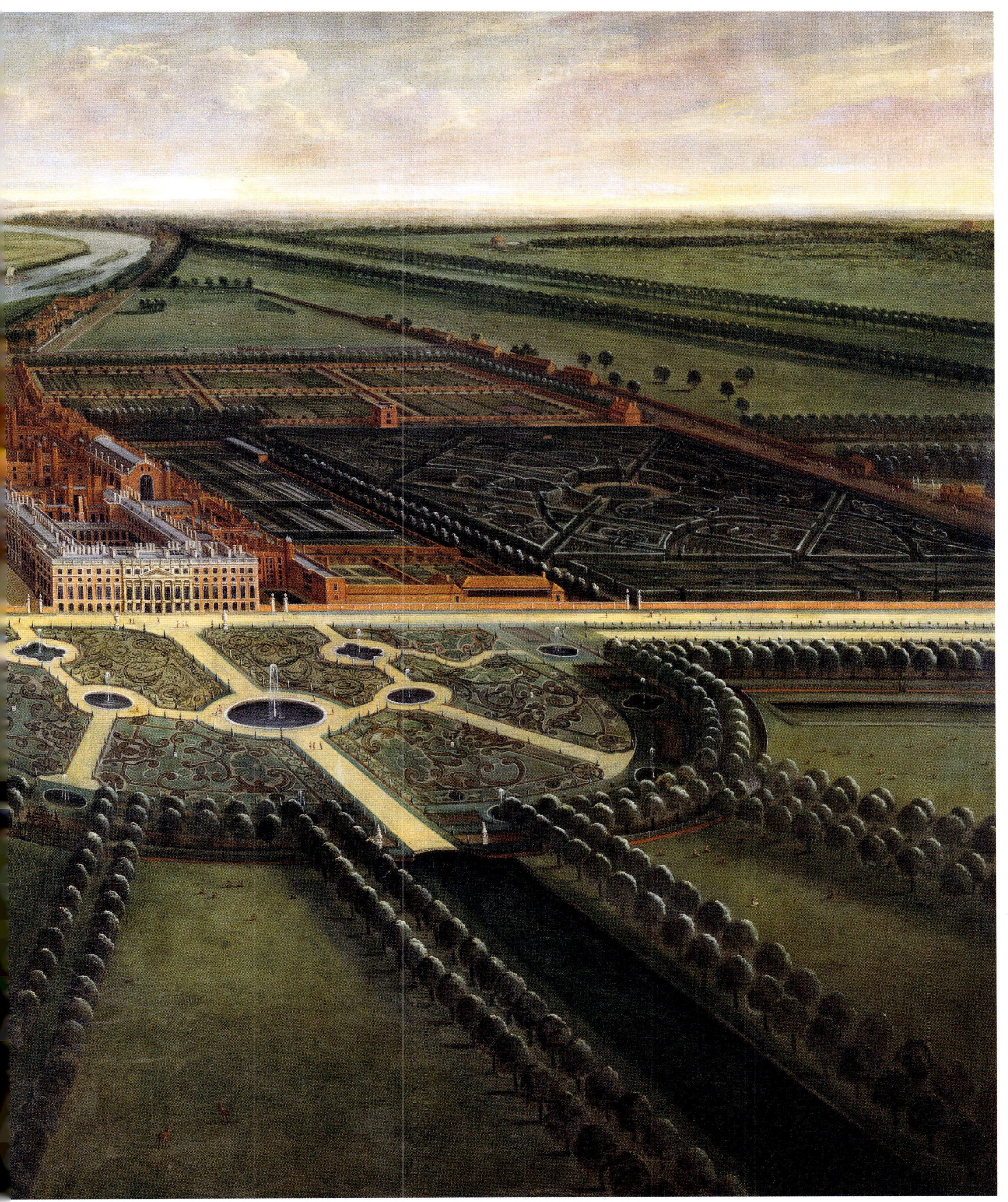

Below Engraver Jan Kip collaborated with the artist Leonard Knyff to record the lavish extent of many great British gardens, but none was more celebrated than those created at Hampton Court Palace by William and Mary.

Opposite The gardens at Bretby Hall, owned by Thomas Coke's father-in-law the Earl of Chesterfield, were vast, elaborate, and generally reputed to be second only to Versailles in their magnificence.

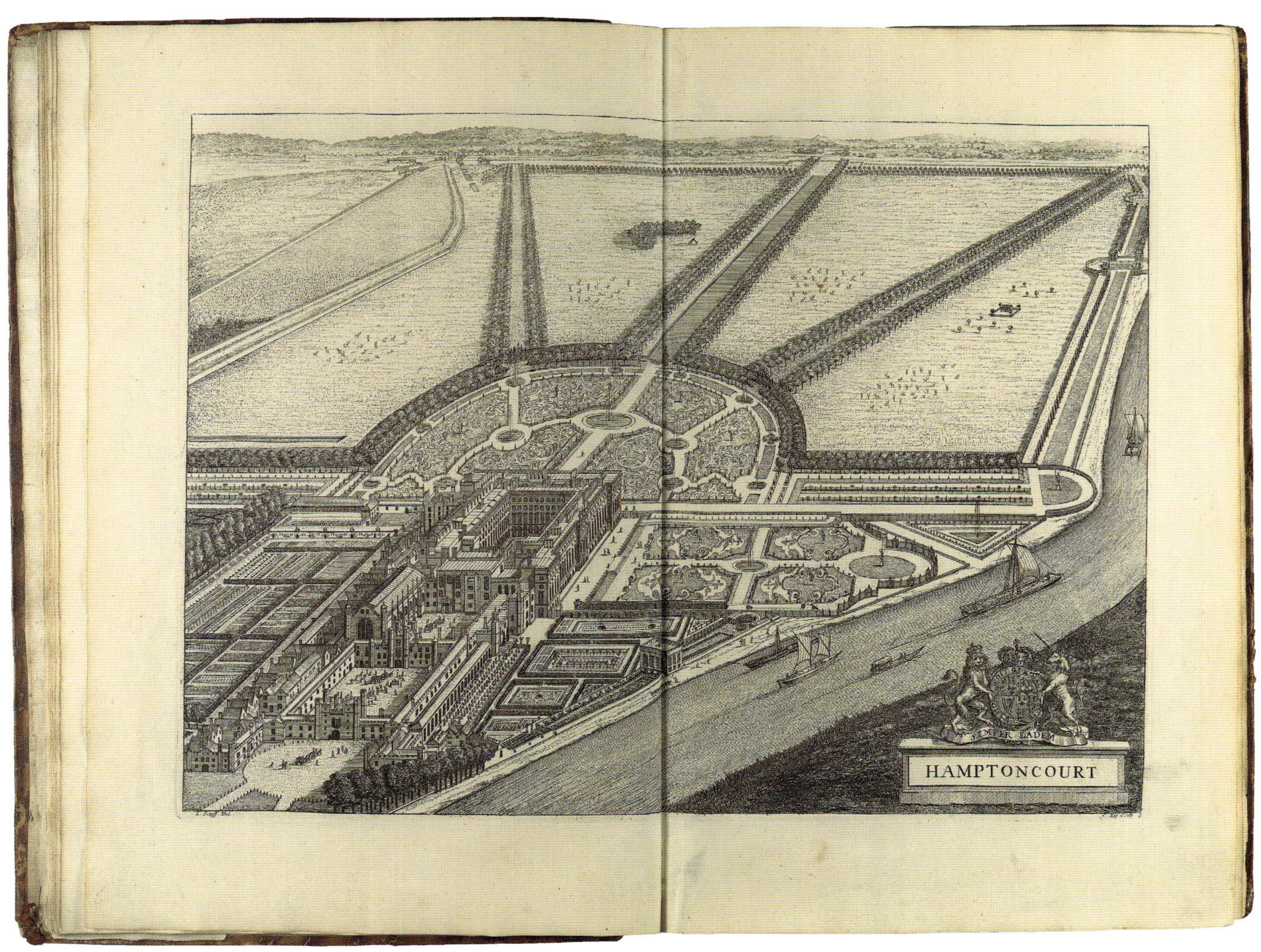

estates were to survive the next big fashion (the faux-natural landscape gardens of Capability Brown and his ilk), but they have been preserved for posterity in the intricate bird's-eye illustrations of Jan Kip and Leonard Knyff that appeared in their famous collaborative work, *Britannia Illustrata*, first published in 1707.

To modern eyes, these drawings of the great estates at Hampton Court and Clandon, amongst many others, look as if their proportions must surely have been exaggerated to flatter the egos of their owners. In fact, recent comparisons made with the actual dimensions of the sites suggest that many are surprisingly accurate, despite their impressive scale. Whether these ostentatious French-style landscapes actually fitted into the more intimate and undulating topography of the English countryside – physically or aesthetically – is another matter entirely. Either way, there were few landowners with access to the vast financial resources necessary to create such extravaganzas.

One person who did have the means and the will to spend lavishly on his garden was the Earl of Chesterfield, who in time would become Thomas Coke's father-in-law. In 1689 he began developing the gardens of his estate at Bretby in the grandest Versailles style, complete with complex parterres, elaborate waterworks and a collection of tender plants that included seventeen lemon cultivars and no less than twenty-three different oranges. In general, however, such extravagant gardens as Bretby and the sixty-nine that featured in *Britannia Illustrata* were notable precisely because they were exceptional. Many other members of the landed nobility had more modest aspirations and, while drawing inspiration from the lavish excesses of the few, created gardens that set out to gently expand the more intimate and domestic scale of their earlier incarnations.

The one thing they all had in common was a rich and varied palette of plants to draw upon. In the hundred years before Thomas inherited Melbourne Hall there had been a huge increase in the number of new species entering Europe for the first time, and this stimulated a renewed interest in the ornamental potential of plant material. Add to this the mania for tree-lined avenues of exceedingly great length and it becomes clear that the fashion opened up some interesting business opportunities for any horticulturally minded individuals enterprising enough to jump on the band wagon. Foremost among these new nurserymen were George London and Henry Wise.

Until around the middle of the seventeenth century, most British landowners wanting to make a garden on a significant scale would have imported their ornamental plants (including bulbs such as tulips, narcissi, anemones and hyacinths) and fruit trees from Holland or northern France. In England there was little equivalent tradition of high-volume plant growing, but that

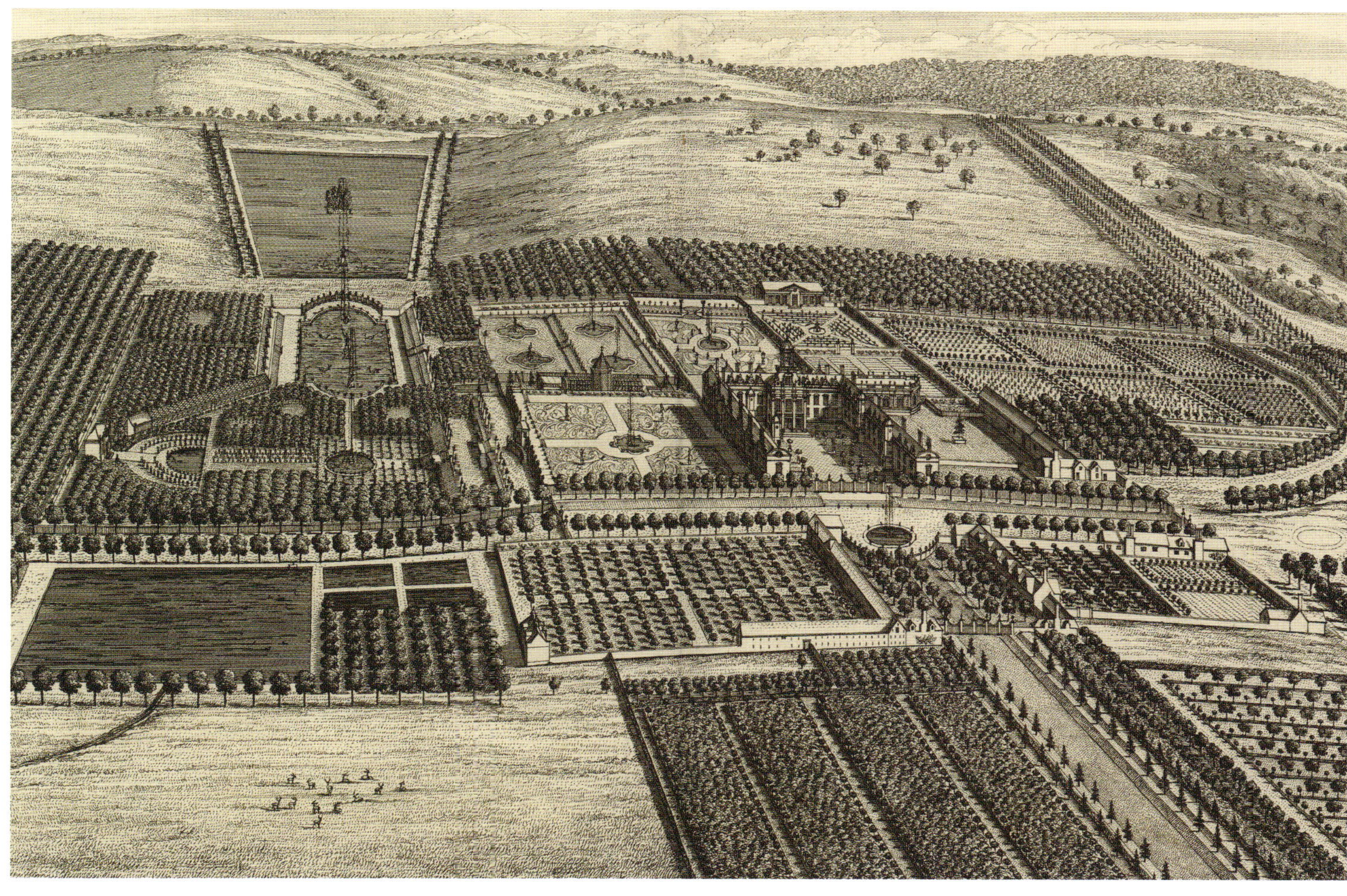

all changed in 1681, when the Brompton Park Nursery opened for business on a vast tract of land in the west of London, roughly where the Victoria & Albert Museum, the Science Museum and the Natural History Museum now stand.

The business was originally set up in 1681 by George London, one time gardener to the plant-mad Bishop of London, Henry Compton, and three other partners. In the following couple of years there was a swift succession of siftings and sortings, and by 1689 the business was jointly owned by London and his former assistant Henry Wise. At this time London was also serving King William III and Queen Mary as their Deputy Gardens Superintendent, and when Queen Anne acceded to the throne in 1702 the royal stamp of approval passed conveniently to Wise, who the new queen appointed as the overall Superintendent of her gardens.

In every respect, the Brompton Park partnership proved to be a supremely successful combination of complementary skills that made the two men extremely rich. Wise preferred to stay in London, managing the day-to-day running of the nursery, corresponding with customers and caring for the gardens of Queen Anne. Meanwhile George London was the travelling face of the business. He made several trips to the continent to keep up with the latest design trends and, from this point onwards, he was almost constantly on the road to meet and consult with the nursery's illustrious list of rural clients. Not only did he take orders to supply them with plants, which were then fulfilled by Wise back in the capital, but he also redesigned many of their gardens in the newly fashionable French manner.

As Stephen Switzer, an eminent garden designer, author and former apprentice of George London wrote in 1715:

> *It will perhaps be hardly believed in time to come, that this one Person actually saw and gave Directions once or twice a Year in most of the Noblemens and Gentlemens Gardens in England. And since it was common for him to ride 50 or 60 Miles in a Day, he made his Northern Circuit in five or six Weeks, and sometimes less; and his Western in as little Time: As for the South and East, they were but three or four Days Work for him.*

One of the 'Gentlemens Gardens' we know he visited was Melbourne Hall, although we also know that pinning him down to a particular date was not an easy matter. Eventually, Thomas and George London met in 1701 on a sloping parcel of land that Thomas was in the process of purchasing with a view to extending his garden; they stood together on the gentle peak to discuss what might best be done with it.

Whether George London also drew up original plans for the design of this new garden area or was simply invited to comment on a set of drawings that had already been developed by Thomas, is a question of ongoing debate in academic circles.

Right Even before he owned the title deeds to all the land within the Melbourne Hall gardens, Thomas Coke spent lavishly on plants, and seems to have had a penchant for narcissi and other spring bulbs.

Opposite There are a number of letters from George London in the Melbourne Hall archives, including this attempt to coordinate a convenient time for him to meet Thomas Coke and discuss ideas for the gardens.

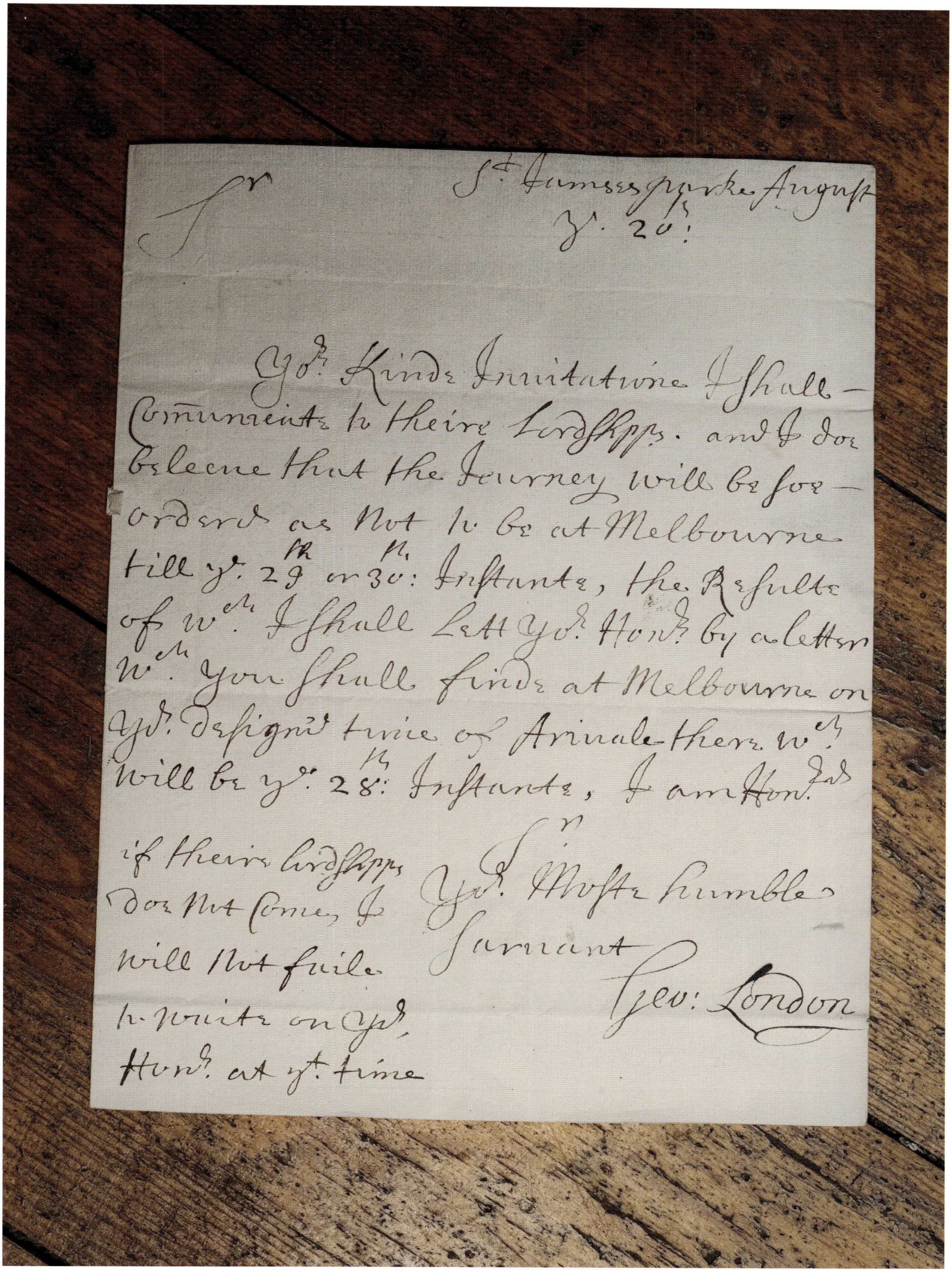

Sr St Jamese parke August
ye 20:

Yor Kinde Inuitatione I shall
Communicate to theire Lordshpps. and I doe
beleeue that the Journey will be soe
ordered as Not to be at Melbourne
till ye 29th or 30th Instante, the Resulte
of wch I shall Lett Yor Honr by a letter
wch you shall finde at Melbourne on
Yor designed time of Arriuale there wch
will be ye 28th Instante, I am Honred

Sr
Yor Moste humble
Seruant
Geo: London

if theire Lordshpps
doe Not Come, I
will Not faile
to waite on Yor
Honr at yt time

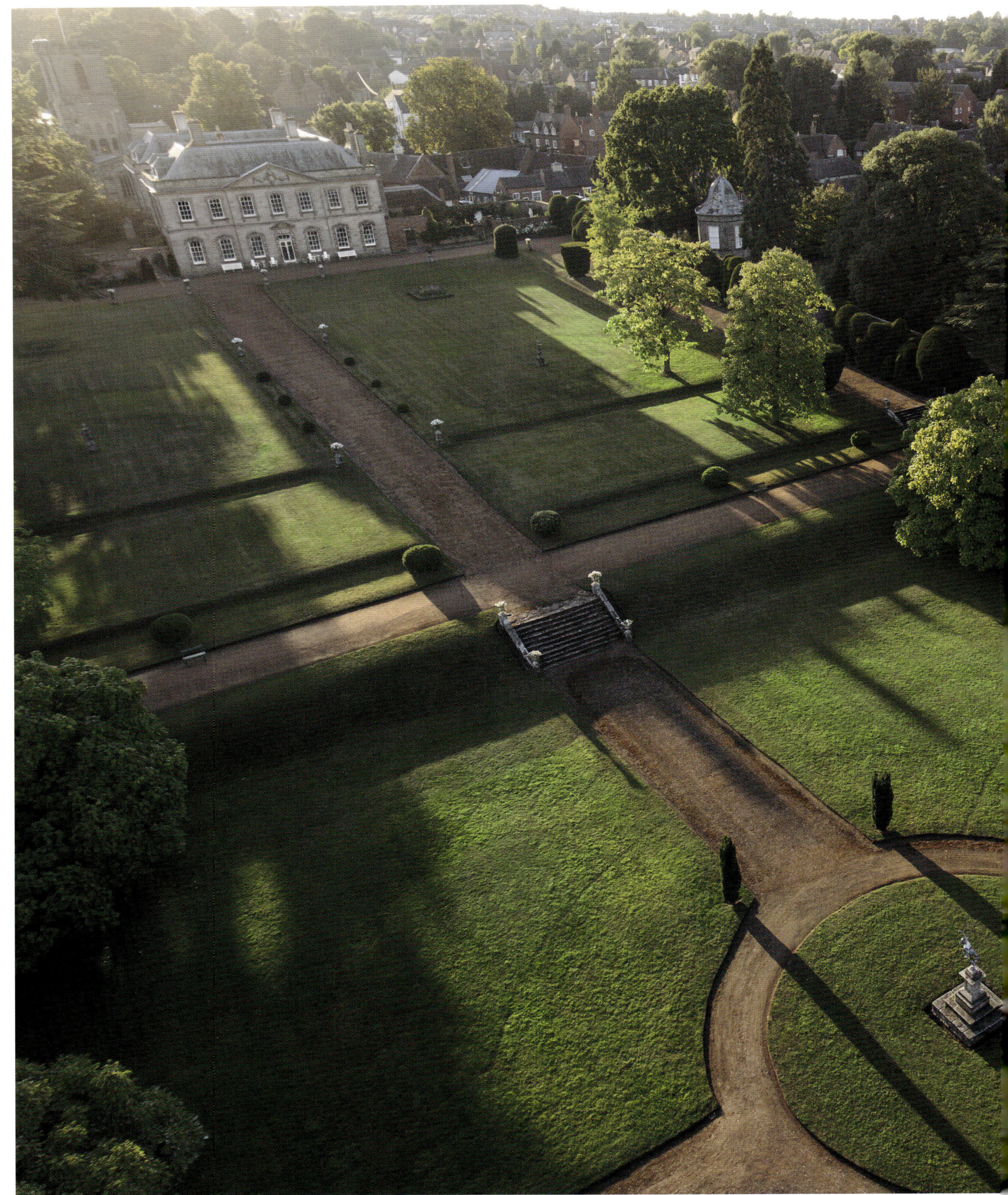

There is a letter in the estate archives sent by Henry Wise, in his role as the office administrator of the business, who wrote to Thomas stating that 'you have chosen the drawing to fit with Versailles', which has been taken by some as evidence that the design did indeed originate with London and Wise. However, there are no items in the estate accounts or archives to support this view and, as garden historian Sally Jeffery has pointed out, this statement should be considered in the light of a letter sent to Thomas by George London in August 1701 discussing potential dates for their site meeting. He writes, 'I may have an opportunity to wait on your Honour in those parts [Melbourne]; so that if you take your draughts with you, we may come to some conclusion there.' This certainly appears to support the view of Thomas's descendants and their archivist that he presented a set of his own original drawings to London and Wise for their professional appraisal.

The one point that is not subject to debate is that only a series of fortunate accidents of history prevented Thomas Coke's garden being swept away by subsequent shifts in fashion, in the way that almost every one of the grand gardens immortalized by Kip and Knyff were subsequently demolished. Consequently, in place of an engraved image, we can still walk in the shade of a great tunnel of yew to the statues, pools and fountains of the glorious garden that Thomas devoted his life to creating.

Left Viewed from the air, the close proximity of the town of Melbourne is striking, providing a busy backdrop that acts as a perfect foil for the calm formality of the gardens.

Chapter 4
Thomas Coke and the Making of His Garden

Opposite Viewed across the still water of the Great Basin, Melbourne Hall is perfectly framed by the arrangement of grass plats, gravel paths, and a tapestry of mature trees.

Thomas was a courtier, a sociable man-about-town and a fond father but, above all, he was a natural-born garden maker.

He seems to have developed a passion for the Melbourne Hall gardens at a young age and, as the first-born son, he grew up knowing that one day he would inherit the estate. As it turned out, Thomas was only seventeen when his father, Colonel John Coke, died in 1692. He had to wait four years before he came of age and could take control of the property, but that didn't dim his enthusiasm. Instead, Thomas passed the time by hatching plans for how best to make his mark on the estate the minute that he was legally able to do so.

In the later seventeenth century, garden making ranked alongside architecture and an appreciation of art and literature as a suitable pursuit for a well-educated young man, but even by the standards of the day Thomas seems to have been more than usually consumed with thoughts about his garden. He kept a number of notebooks that today are stored in the estate archives – their covers slightly softened with age but the writing inside still bold and clear – in which he jotted down many ideas for expansion and elaboration, *aides memoires*, observations and notes on plants he had seen and admired elsewhere.

Clearly, he was keen to start work, but even when he did legally inherit, Thomas was unable to immediately implement his plans for enlarging and remodelling the gardens, because the house and part of its grounds were still only held on lease from the Bishop of Carlisle. None of his bigger ideas could sensibly be realized until he was in possession of the freehold, but in 1698, as a first step to regularizing the situation, he commissioned a plan. This showed what land he already owned and what was still the property of the bishop; today it serves as a useful record of the garden layout before he started work, with the 'Dove Cote' (now the Muniment Room) clearly labelled as a useful benchmark.

The negotiations were protracted by various stumbling blocks that had to be overcome, but eventually terms were agreed that satisfied both parties. In all, it took some six years for the matter to be concluded but, in the meantime, Thomas couldn't resist some instant gratification. Between 1696 and 1699 he placed a number of large plant orders with the celebrated Brompton Park Nursery owned by George London and Henry Wise, and the estate archive contains many receipts, signed in the hand of Henry Wise, which show the vast scale on which Thomas purchased trees, shrubs, flowers and bulbs in that period.

One single docket, within a large bundle of letters and bills in one of the many archived boxes of correspondence, gives a good indication of how lavishly Thomas was prepared to spend on his garden at that time. It includes many dozens of peaches and nectarines, thirty-two cherry trees, four apricots and twenty-four figs, plus long lists of 'Things had of ye Seedsman'. Among an awful lot else, this rollcall of assorted salad, herb, vegetable and ornamental seeds mentions several kinds of basil, candytuft, French marigold and sweet scabious seed, amaranthus, convolvulus, lupins, 'Mixt Tulip Roots', double jonquils, double ranunculus and double anemones. The order concluded with a request for '2 Garden Hoes, 2 Garden Sythes . . . a lock for ye Garden gate . . . 20 Orange Trees; Some Honeysuckles in balls . . . 4 fine Arbutus Trees These for Edging . . . and . . . 100 Tubyrose Roots'.

It was an expensive exercise, but Thomas was no careless spendthrift. He cared as deeply about the proper maintenance of his existing gardens as he did about buying new plants and plotting future improvements, and he was constantly on the lookout for good ideas to borrow from the gardens of his friends.

Among many notebooks in the archives is one with a marbled paper cover, neatly inscribed in Thomas's handwriting with the title: 'Notes and Memorandums concerning my gardens – 1698'. This includes a list dated 1 December of 'Things to be done this winter in my garden while I am away', which largely focussed on hedges and fruit, but also included the making of a melon bed. A few pages on, Thomas writes himself a memo 'To make a little grove of trees on ye left hand of the Lower garden fit to walk in to make thicketts in it of Roses of several sorts and hony suckles . . . and what it was Haris planted at Windsor which grew up soe very fast to be a shade.'

His biggest conundrum, in an era of formal symmetry, was that the central axis of his garden was very noticeably not centred on his house. Maybe he would have preferred to start with a blank canvas of flat, open land and the possibility of setting out fashionably extensive axes and vistas on all sides, but this part of Derbyshire is gently hilly, and his property was (and still is) closely wrapped by the town of Melbourne. The parish church sits hard by the main gates, and, in Thomas's time, public roads ran around at least half the total perimeter of the site, which meant his room for manoeuvre was decidedly limited.

In theory, at least, these 'problems' could have been overcome. Just twenty years later when his close namesake Sir Thomas Coke of Holkham Hall, in the county of Norfolk (who was not actually a relation), began work on improving his own estate he, too, was faced with the problem of uncomfortably close neighbours. His solution was to begin a process that ended with the destruction and wholesale removal of the village of Holkham, which had so inconveniently thwarted his vision for the wider landscape.

In contrast, Thomas eventually decided to enhance what already existed rather than sweeping it all away and starting completely afresh. Some of the property surrounding the Hall was not in his control, and perhaps his pockets were not deep enough to negotiate all the purchases that would have been necessary. As a result, the layout of the garden today

demonstrates a clear and relatively gentle progression from that shown in the plan drawn up for his great grandfather in 1629.

In 1699, Thomas sent his own design for the garden to Henry Wise, who in turn consulted with George London, freshly returned from France, where he had been studying a number of Le Nôtre's gardens. With the approval of these celebrated experts to reassure him that his ideas were sound, Thomas set his bailiff John Payne to work.

In a memorandum 'about Levelling ye Garden' dated 25 November 1699, written in Thomas's sloping hand, Payne is contracted to:

Opposite The Muniment Room, then called the 'Dove Cote', clearly marked on the plan of Melbourne Hall commissioned by Thomas Coke in 1698 before he started work on the gardens, is now the backdrop to a charming little Winter Garden.

Above On bright and frosty mornings, the simple formality at the heart of the gardens is shown off to great effect by the low slanting of winter shadows.

Left The fragrance of a careful selection of winter-flowering shrubs, including this lovely honeysuckle (*Lonicera fragrantissima*) fills the air in the Winter Garden on still, cold mornings.

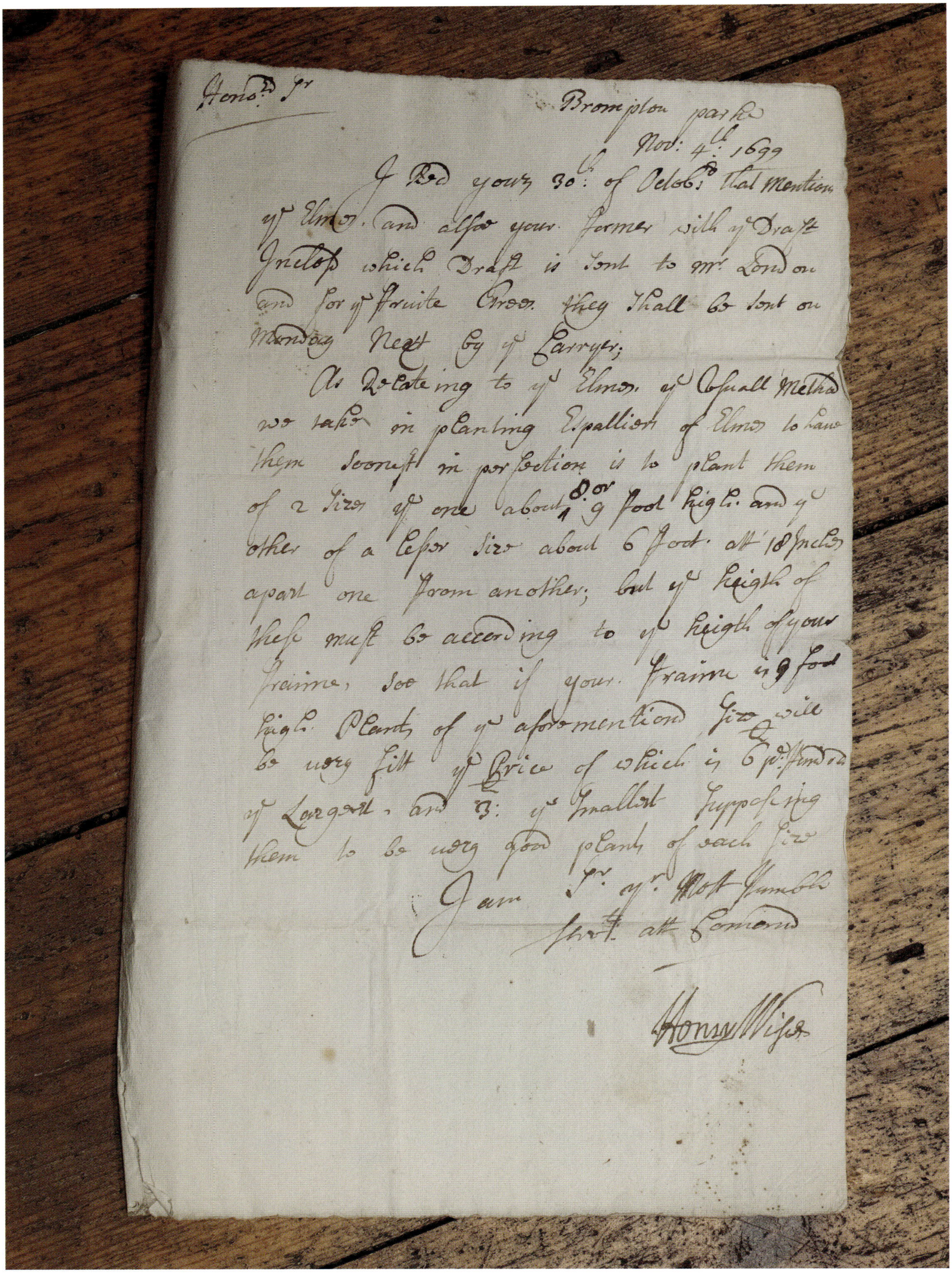

Hond Sr

Brompton parke
Nov: 4th 1699

I Recd yours 30th of Octob: that mention
ye Elms. and alsoe your former with ye Draft
Inclosd which Draft is sent to Mr London
and for ye fruite Trees they shall be sent on
Monday Next by ye Carryer;

As Relateing to ye Elms. ye Usuall Method
we take in planting Espalliers of Elms to have
them soonest in perfection is to plant them
of 2 sizes ye one about 8 or 9 foot high and ye
other of a lesser size about 6 foot att 18 Inches
apart one from another; but ye heigth of
these must be according to ye heigth of your
fraime, soe that if your fraime is 9 foot
high Plants of ye aformention Size will
be very fitt ye Price of which is 6 pd. Hundred
ye Largest, and 3: ye smallest supposeing
them to be very good plants of each size

I am Sr yr Most humble
Servt. att Command

Henry Wise

. . . level the Islands within the motes and slope the sides of them, and make the walks round the motes all but the long walk that goes along by the brook side of an exact level as far as is sett out and likewise the walks round the fountains within the Espalier. He is likewise to make two fountains slop'd with green turf.

In exchange for this work, and the laying of a complicated network of pipes between the various water features, Thomas agreed to pay him 'tenn pounds in hand, tenn pounds att Christmas, tenn pounds att Candlemass, and tenn pounds att the finishing of the work'.

In addition, the old fish ponds were modified, the lower garden layout was refined and two additional stone-edged pools with fountains were constructed. Today these are known as the Round Grass Fountain and the South Stone Fountain, which contains the 'little boy called Triton', although this lead statue was not added until later.

By 1701, Thomas had also produced a masterplan for the rest of the garden that he discussed with George London during a site visit in October of that year. As a result, when Thomas finally gained the freehold to his land by an Act of Parliament in 1704 he was ready to start work straight away.

The man he chose to implement his ideas was the gardener William Cooke of Walcot, who had already worked on a number of the grander estates in the area. Cooke was contracted to reconstruct the old flower and kitchen gardens as 'a division of Partare work' with 'terrasses, sloops, Verges and fleets of steps', for the sum of £400. The plans included decorating the grass parterres flanking the broad central path with ornamental cutwork, standard trees and statuary. This whole symmetrical arrangement was to be bordered on the north side by a single yew hedge, and to the south by a double hedge trained over a wooden frame to form a pleasantly shaded walkway.

The major works began in May 1704, just a few months after Thomas's first wife, Mary, had died and, since his position at court demanded he spend most of his time in London, he left the overseeing of the project – as well as the day-to-day care of the estate and of his two young daughters – in the capable hands of his sister Betsy. Over a great number of neatly written pages she recorded the day-to-day conversations, instructions and tribulations of this elaborate endeavour, which could so easily have been lost, but instead have been magically preserved in the bulging estate archives. As a result, we know that William Cooke positively sprang into action, and the gardens were soon filled with workmen and all their associated noise and dust. We also know that Betsy's patience was often sorely tried by all the commotion.

Even so, by the beginning of June, William Cooke was making good progress and reporting back to his employer that 'ye works . . . [were] in as great a forwardness as the time will permit'. By July he was ready to install the statues that Thomas

Opposite Henry Wise, as the office-based half of the London & Wise partnership, corresponded regularly with Thomas Coke about his lavish plant orders. Many of those letters are still preserved within the Melbourne Hall archives.

Left Exploring the Melbourne Hall archives is an exciting exercise, producing centuries-old plans folded in between correspondence, receipts and work orders.

had purchased from Jan van Nost's fashionable workshop at Hyde Park Corner. These included magnificent statues of Perseus and Andromeda, two fine figures personifying the continents of Africa and Asia, and a number of playful cherubs (which were initially set out along the lawns in the upper and lower parterres but were subsequently moved to other locations within the gardens).

Having improved his existing gardens as far as was possible, Thomas was eager to realize his ambition to expand the wider boundaries of his property, and in October 1704 he drew up a second contract with William Cooke to lay out a new series of gardens on an adjacent plot of land for the sum of £450, including levelling the ground for 'divisions of wilderness work', 'reservoirs or bassons for water', fruit walls, kitchen gardens, orchards, plantations and hedged alleys. It was not the easiest site, being offset to the southeast of the existing garden and out of sight of the house, with a gentle slope rising to its midpoint, but it was his only possibility for enlargement.

The practicalities of the work, as set down in that contract, give a sense of the enormous scale of the undertaking, with itemized tasks including:

1st Division – £75 5s
Trenching, levelling etc the division next the Arbour – £25
Trenching and levelling the Potagery – £6
Digging and planting etc the Alder Grove – £35
Trenching and making up borders in Dog Kennel & Bleaching Yard – £5
Sinking the Reservoir, raising and ramming the slopes & making borders – £175 17s
Digging and working the Mill Close, and making it into Kitchen Gdn – £108 10s
Sinking and making ye Reservoir, as in draft – £19 8s

Equally challenging, though harder to quantify, were the aesthetics of the project. Inspired by the great formal gardens he had visited on his travels through France, Thomas could see how well a series of wilderness walks would fit within this wedge-shaped piece of land and he worked with Cooke to devise a network of paths that were cleverly designed to set up a sequence of constantly cross-referencing vistas, anchored by an elegant series of slender fountains and carved urns.

Nearly one hundred years later, Thomas's great-granddaughter Emily, who herself owned Melbourne Hall for a while, wrote

Right As the household consumption of home-grown fruit and vegetables has reduced over the years, parts of the kitchen garden have been modified into a decorative potager, with a young *Crataegus orientalis* planted at its heart.

Left The pale and extremely pretty iris which now fills one cut-flower bed in the kitchen garden is a previously unknown variety discovered at Melbourne, which has been named *Iris* 'Melbourne Hall Ghost'.

that the 'fountains which flow perpetually are seen from so many different vistas that you think the number doubled. The dark walks and yew hedges are also beautiful.' Even today, the effect is pleasingly confusing for first-time visitors, and helps to make the gardens feel much bigger than they are in reality.

At the highest point of the new parcel of land, Cooke drew out a *patte d'oie*, which translates literally as 'goose foot' and describes an arrangement of avenues radiating out from a centre point. As the name suggests, this was a feature made popular by the grander French gardens, but it also happened to be perfectly suited to this rolling corner of the English countryside. The design device translated well into Melbourne Hall's more intimate scale and, with its strong diagonal element, made the most of this troublesomely offset plot, presenting a range of alternative routes to lure walkers away from the central parterre and out into the newly acquired wider grounds.

The Four Seasons Urn, a magnificent gift reputed to have been given to Thomas by Queen Anne, was positioned at the very centre of the *patte d'oie*, giving suitable prominence to this finest of the van Nost pieces in the garden. The avenues that radiated out from this centre point were laid to turf and flanked by tall lime and hornbeam hedges that enclosed 'wilderness' areas filled with yet more trees and flowering shrubs.

The plan that William Cooke created to illustrate these interconnecting elements has been preserved in the archives. It is beautifully drawn, with a notably delicate penmanship, but it has been overlaid with a series of energetic, rough lines. It is easy to imagine that these were added by Thomas in the course of an animated conversation between the two men about how the garden would actually work on the ground.

Some of their design elements were purely practical, such as the three long brick walls that were built to provide warm, south-facing surfaces against which fruit trees could be trained. Other features were purely decorative, including the impressive Great Basin that replaced the old moated islands with a single body of water, and was the closest approximation to a fashionable canal or 'Long Water' that Thomas could accommodate on the site.

According to an entry in his notebook, Thomas originally planned to position a large statuary group in the centre of this pool: 'In ye midst of ye great piece of water, a Venus coming out of the Sea, standing on a piece of rockwork, and four nymphs at ye corners of ye rock. Ye rockwork to be like that under Neptune at Vaux le Vicomte.' With the perspective of 300 years hindsight, the absence of this excitable piece of stonework feels like no great loss, although it would be interesting to know why Thomas eventually changed his mind.

It is unlikely to have been a question of economy. Thomas was not only spending lavishly on materials and labour at this stage, but he also hadn't curtailed his plant-buying habits in the slightest. Take as an example the astonishing receipt from Henry Wise dated 1705/6 that, in addition to even more plums, cherries, pears, peaches and nectarines, includes: '59 Vines at 6d . . . 71 flowering Shrubs on each side of ye Arbor', plus hundreds of roses, honeysuckles, hollyhocks and 'Persian Jessamines'. Also on the list, among a great deal more, were 50 wild service trees, 20 wild olives, 100 laburnums, 100 guelder roses, 50 lilacs, 1,000 'shrubs' and hundreds more trees for 'ye hedge Lines' and large numbers of hardy evergreens, including pyramid yews and holly, 45 m (50 yd) of dwarf box and 8 round-headed 'True phillarees'. 'Flower Rootes for ye Lower Ground' included 50 each of orange and white lilies, Turk's cap lilies and Crown imperials, hundreds of irises, tulips and white narcissus, plus crocus, snowdrops and hyacinths in great quantities. This single bill alone amounted to £445 1s 5d, which is equivalent to more than £86,000 today.

Given the huge number of plants that were constantly being transported from London to Melbourne, it is all the more impressive that by 22 March 1705 William Cooke was writing to Thomas at his home in St James's Place, London, to declare: 'I have now completed all our planting hear & by to morrow night the Walk from the Bottom of the piece of Water to the Octagon in the Mill Close will be completely Turf with the Circular & other Basons wch looks extreamly well'. Work on the various water features was also ongoing and he reported that 'its now a very good Season for the Conveyance of the Wast Water from ye fountain' and that he had been consulting with George Sorrocold about the most efficient way of proceeding.

By July 1705 Betsy was writing to Thomas with relief to say:

All the dust and noisy work of your gardens is finished, the gravel walks being done. I believe you will be much pleased with them, and these late rains have refreshed the turfs and the trees, that you will find it in great beauty. They are now making the arches to the bason and coping the wall round it. The little fountains are done with stone, and they have begun to level the ground in the larger grove.

By the following year, the traumatic upheaval of the building phase was fading from Betsy's mind as she wrote to Thomas to let him know how successfully the young gardens had settled down:

Indeed your gardens are more than pleasant. And there is the plantation of the elm arbor, which I am sure will surprise you by its growth. The greens in general are in a very thriving way this year, and with very little pains of watering. I suppose Mr Cooke has been with you, and therefore I might have spared my account; but you know my infirmity of scribbling.

William Cooke certainly did maintain a proprietorial eye on proceedings. As late as October 1706, when work on the garden was essentially completed, he continued to keep a sharp eye on its development. On 18 October 1706 he wrote to Thomas in St James's Place with an update on the establishment of the most

recent phase of planting which, he said, was 'in as good order as I could expect . . . the Greens grow very well onley one yew in the partare is dead. The fruit trees & vines have shott very well & some of the latter bore good grapes . . . we have had also extraordinary good figs.' But while Cooke was concerned to secure the finishing touches, including '20 yards of good fresh box to fill up the edgings before the frost comes', Robert Bakewell was only just starting work on the crowning glory of the garden as we know it today.

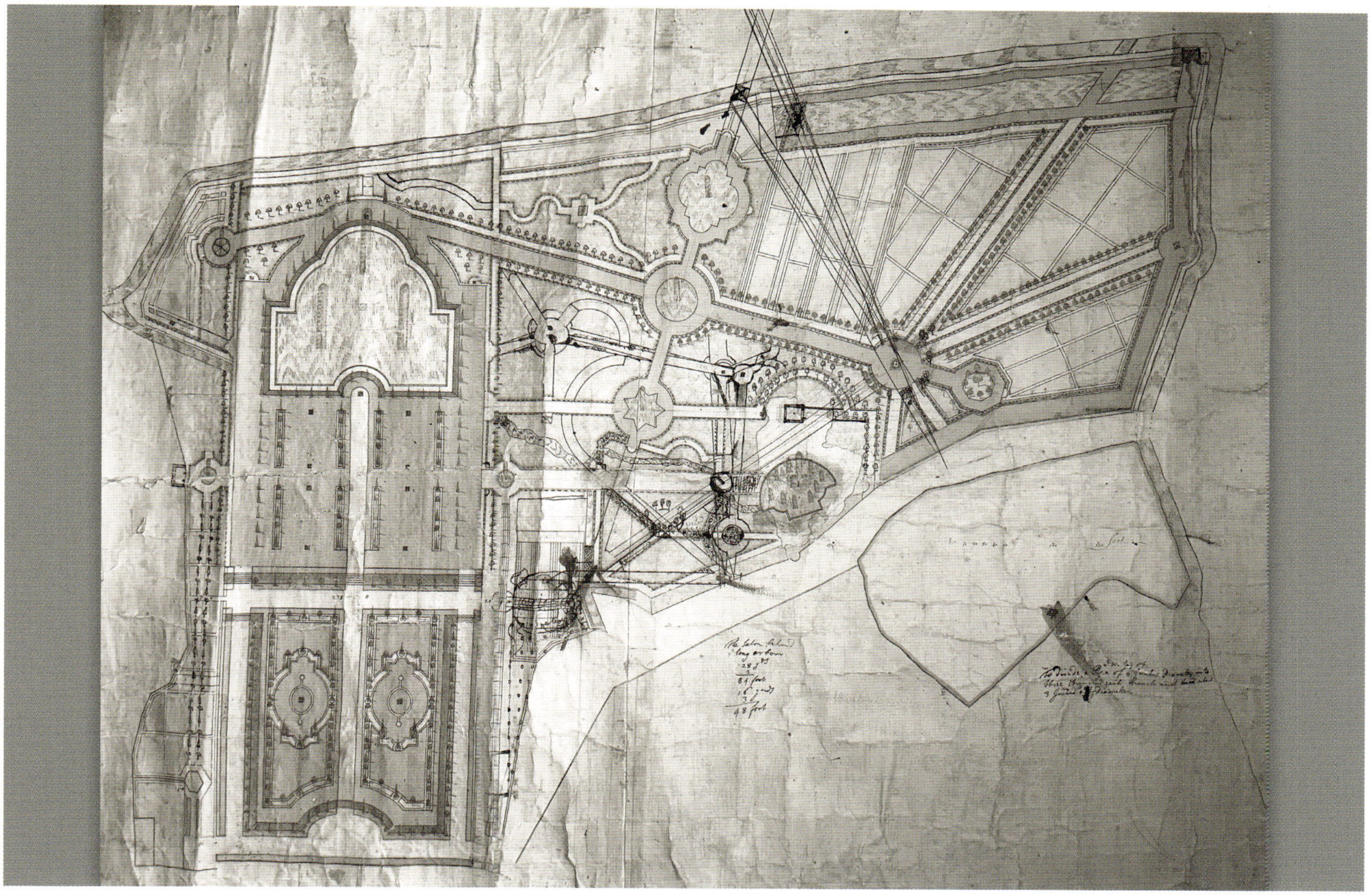

Bakewell arrived in 1706 and spent the next two years creating the elaborate wrought-iron Birdcage, working at a forge in the basement of the building known as Stone House, next to the parish church. For this monumental undertaking he was paid £120, a figure he had agreed to at the start of the project,

Above A finely drawn plan of the gardens produced in Thomas Coke's day clearly shows the clever rationalization of his extended gardens, using vistas, axes and a *patte d'oie* on the highest point.

Left Turk's cap lilies (*Lilium martagon*), with their preference for dappled shade, are planted in the cooler, woodland areas of the garden today, as they were in the seventeenth century

Above The Muniment Room, formerly the 'Dove Cote', is one of the first features that visitors encounter as they begin to stroll down Library Walk.

Opposite The details of the garden disappear under a blanket of snow, but the structural elements still clearly define the formal layout of the space.

but which turned out to be a serious underestimate of the true cost of the work. By the time this magnificent piece was finished, in 1708, Bakewell was virtually destitute, but the Birdcage made him famous, and he went on to become recognized as one of the finest blacksmiths in the country.

Bakewell was a refined craftsman, but his personal habits were decidedly coarse, and Betsy found him a rather disreputable and undesirable character. Even so, she was fascinated by his work, and wrote to tell Thomas all about visiting the forge. 'I was just to see your iron work which is certainly very fine, & a great curiosity to see the manner of their doeing it, he sais he shall now soon have finish't it.' In the same letter, she reports that:

> *I don't know what to say of your Gardens bar as I use to doe, mighty pleasant and sweet, & as to the keeping very few faults to be found, and we have sufficient plenty of what is nesisary in them, not but that when you come you will find a great many things both in the gardens & out, that would be rectified by a masters eye over them.*

Despite overseeing the day-to-day maintenance, Betsy never lost sight of the fact that it was Thomas's garden, although on occasion she did instigate some small improvements of her own. These were invariably practical, not aesthetic, and included setting one of the estate workers to 'catching some pikes to put in the great Bason, for I thought it was great pity to have year after year pass without any stock in it.'

Towards the end of 1709, Betsy was updating Thomas on the changes that had been begun in 1708 to convert the old dovecot into a Muniment Room where he could house his books. This involved raising the height of the building and remodelling it according to an original design developed by Thomas to produce the distinctive ogee-shaped roofline that is such an attractive feature of the gardens today. The conversion could ultimately be declared a great success but, like almost every other building project in history, along the way it became disruptive, delayed and somewhat over budget. 'Your library has been finished some time, but is not dry yet,' she wrote. 'I believe it will not be fit to be ventured with your writings till summer, when I hope you will come to place them yourself. I believe you will like the room in all respect, but the cost.'

By March the following year, 1710, things had settled down to such an extent that Betsy wrote to her brother that although 'I have not been round your Garden a great while' the estate staff were reporting that they had 'very near finished all the plantations'.

Throughout the long years of the project, Thomas and Betsy between them had displayed an admirable ability to choose and manage their staff very well, but even they could not control the weather, and a few months later the elements hit the newly established garden hard. In a letter dated 8 May 1710 Betsy wrote that:

Your garden is kept in seeming good order, and no want in the kitchen garden. But you will find a very great change in the beauty of your greens in the Parterre by last year and this also. About six weeks ago they began to promise recovery in a great measure; but the same cold winds that have taken away the fruit have strangely struck the Phyllereas that was left alive: and the laurels seem some of them to be quite killed. The yews and the round hollies are well, but the spire hollies, some of them, look but ill: whether this has come from any neglect to them, I cannot judge.

Her words conjure a picture of a richly planted young garden in which the expensive new topiary pieces were proving highly susceptible to the elements. Any keen gardener will sympathize. While interior decoration incurs a considerable degree of expense and upheaval when it is being installed, the finished rooms are at least guaranteed to look good for many years to come. In contrast, the exterior decoration of the garden designer is considerably more vulnerable to pest, disease and the worst nature can throw at it.

Thomas understood that no garden can ever be declared complete and, even when the main programme of work was finally concluded, he continued to make refinements. Some of these decisions had quite an impact, including the reorganization of his collection of van Nost cherub statues, which eventually found their way to the hedge niches where they still nestle today.

Thomas was still primarily based in London, but he seems to have been almost constantly issuing detailed instructions about every minute aspect of the care of his beloved gardens. A letter written by him on 29 September 1722 to Mr Shepherd, his agent, gives some sense of the degree to which he micromanaged from a distance:

. . . you must take care to let the ground be dug turn'd at least two foot deep before you plant, tho' you have plow'd it; you'll begin planting as soon as there hath been a little rain, remember to water and mulch ye Trees as soon as you have planted, and it being uphill I believe it will be best to carry thither ye Engine and Pipes . . . In ye Catalogue of ye fruit I don't see any Catharine peach if I have any send them up. The Beune pears should be put up immediately lay them up in paper & take care they bee not bruis'd.

Mr Shepherd, in his turn, wrote to Thomas on 5 December 1722 with an update which makes it clear that he still had an awful lot more than the wrapping of pears to occupy his time.

Sir . . . this morning [I] began to plant the New Intake in the Parkes with Oakes and hope they will doe well for they will be

planted in as good ground and soyle as any Forrest Tree need be the Plants are all about fifteene feet high and that ground will take four hundred oakes besides what more Oakes and Ashes I shall put in the Valleys and hills in the Quarrys. There will be less for a nother year betwixt eight and Nine hundred more Oakes of the same size besides a thousand small ones which was sent for London which doe well.

I received about a fortnight agoe twenty Elmes unpruned I desire to know where you would be pleased to have them sett Out. I received 100 Pippins noe backing Apples as you rought me word.

Inevitably, by the time the surrounding parkland had been filled with trees, the ornamental gardens were already in need of some reorganization and restoration. Two years before his death, Thomas was receiving updates from the indefatigable Mr Shepherd about the Yew Tunnel. On 21 April 1725 he wrote:

Sir - The Frame to the Green Arbour is soe old and rotten that a great part of it is fallen downe and the rest I have been takeing downe for fear it should fall upon some body and kill them as they walke under it . . . when the Wind blowes pretty high . . . the Arbour rocks and shakes all to pieces And to make a new Frame would cost at least a hundred pounds. I am therefore thinking if you approve of it to set downe all the old posts that will doe againe a bout three feet in the ground to make them stand as strong as I can and about 8 or 9 feet against the side of the Arbour upon the Top of the posts and think that will be a great streng[t]hing to it and will not cost much for I believe I can make railes that will doe out of the old Ferr tree that stood I the Poole Garden if you have noe other use for it . . . I designe to tye the top of the Arbour with horse haire to trye if that will hold it for the Crowne of the Frame is almost all fallen the sooner you please to give me your thoughts upon this the better.

There is something magical about this letter, coloured as it is by care, consideration and, reading between the lines, a mutual respect between the agent who cared for Melbourne Hall's gardens day by day and the garden owner who dreamed them into existence and gave so many of his waking hours to planning their enhancement and improvement.

Two years later Mr Shepherd wrote a note, dated 24 May 1727, answering an instruction 'That Mr Sh. make up as soon as he can his Account to ye time of the Death of his late Master.' Thomas's work on his gardens had finally come to an end.

Left Grass, hedges and carefully maintained trees comprise much of the decorative effect in the formal heart of the garden.

The Visitors

Opposite Garden visiting has always been a national pastime, although in the centuries before rural roads were navigable by carriage, the horticulturally curious would have arrived by horseback.

It is easy to get the impression that garden visiting only really began in the twentieth century, with motor cars and cream teas, but visitors have always been welcome at Melbourne Hall. In fact, it was customary in the seventeenth and early eighteenth century for complete strangers – assuming they were of a suitable social standing – to arrive at any of the great estates and ask to be shown around both house and garden. If they were unknown to the family, it would be left to the senior servants to assess their acceptability, negotiate a suitable financial compensation and conduct the tour, but the level of access this would buy you is rather startling by modern standards.

Celia Fiennes was an English traveller and diarist of this era who made many tours of the country, usually riding side saddle because at that time most roads would have been little more than muddy tracks full of potholes and therefore impossible to navigate in a wheeled carriage. As she went along, Celia found time to record her experiences and observations in a series of journals that were eventually published and now provide us with a unique insight into the past and the daily norms of life in her time.

In 1697 she set out to explore the northern counties, including Derbyshire, which, she complained, was 'full of steep hills, and nothing but the peakes of hills as thick one by another is seen in most of the County which are very steepe which makes travelling tedious, and the miles long.' The only saving grace was that this was also the year in which a law was passed requiring each parish to place a fingerpost waymarker at every remote crossroads, so at least she could feel confident that she was travelling in the right direction, however slow her progress might be.

Undaunted by the hardships of the road, Celia records how she arrived at Bretby, home of the Earl of Chesterfield, in the days immediately following the marriage of the Rt. Hon. Thomas Coke to Mary, the eldest daughter of the house. The main purpose of her visit was to explore the gardens, which were renowned for their excellence (and must surely have been an inspiration to the garden-mad young Thomas as he hatched his plans for Melbourne Hall). However, she was also distracted by the ongoing nuptial celebrations, which at that time typically involved the young couple honeymooning in the home of the bride's parents.

Celia was shown round much of the house, including the bridal bedchamber (where she admired the quality of the red velvet bed hangings). As she records it:

> *. . . the drawing roome had company in it – the Earle having just marry'd his eldest Daughter Lady Mary to one Mr. Cooke, a Gentleman of a good Estate hard by, so there was company to wishe her joy – but I was in several bedchambers, one had a crimson damask bed, the other crimson velvet set upon halfe paces, this best was the bride chamber which used to be call'd the Silver roome.*

Her recollections of the ornate gardens at Bretby were recorded in evocative detail, including descriptions of a great number of elaborate fountains and water features, most notably 'a Clock which by the water worke is moved and strikes the hours and chimes the quarters, and when they please play Lilibolaro [a sprightly folk tune which is still performed today] on the Chymes'.

Whatever he thought of his in-laws in general, Thomas doesn't seem to have been tempted to mimic the more elaborate excesses of their gardens. Instead, we can get a better sense of the atmosphere he was probably trying to create at Melbourne Hall by reading Celia Fiennes' description of the gardens at Ingestre in Staffordshire, which she visited shortly after exploring Bretby. Here she enjoyed:

> *. . . gravell walkes full of flowers and greens and a box hedge cut finely with little trees . . . out of this goes into a flower garden divided into knotts . . . thence into another garden with gravel walks and so into a summer house through which you enter a good bowling-green . . . [and] a very fine wilderness with many large walks of a great length, full of all sorts of trees sycamores willows hazel chestnuts walnuts set very thicke and so shorn smooth to the top which is left as a tuff or crown, they are very lofty in growth which makes the length of the walke look nobly.*

Celia never got a chance to visit Melbourne Hall, but there was another adventurous female exploring the country on horseback in the late seventeenth and early eighteenth century who did pay the Coke residence a visit not long after the main work in the gardens was completed. Cassandra Willoughby's journal shows that she had a particular interest in the gardens of all the estates she visited, and her enthusiasm still shines out from the page, allowing us to experience a contemporary appreciation of gardens that today often only exist on paper, if at all.

In 1710, she visited the relatively young gardens at Melbourne Hall, and appears to have been thoroughly impressed by the property, if not by its location:

> *We went to Mr Coke's House at Melbourn which stands but ill in a poor Town. The Gardens are very handsome. On one Side of the Par Terre Garden is a close walk which leads to the Wilderness. This walk they told us had been made but 5 years and was then a perfect shade. The most extraordinary thing I observed in that Garden was an Arbour or Summer-house made of very neat Iron work, which needs being covered with Wood to be shady. A Cascaid and many additions were designed to this Garden.*

We know that no such water feature was ever actually created at Melbourne Hall, but the original garden plan of 1704 does show a proposed cascade in the former quarry site that is now known as the Dell. From this, we can conclude that Cassandra's guided tour of the estate included plenty of general chitchat, behind-the-scenes exploration and a chance to look through the archive of garden plans.

In 1789, the gardens were also visited by John Byng, Viscount Torrington, who set down his observations in his famous travel journal. By this date, most fine formal gardens had been swept away by followers of Capability Brown's pastoral designs, and Byng described Melbourne Hall as 'a decent mansion with such an old fashioned garden of yew hedges, fountains, and alleys, as now becomes a curiosity, and to be admired for that shade so much wanted in modern shrubberies. There is also an interspersion of walled garden where we ate for the first time of cherries.'

This custom of unofficial visits gradually fell from favour in the late eighteenth century, partly because improvements in the quality of the road network and the comfort of carriages meant the number of potential visitors began to increase to unsustainable levels. The great houses were still not completely closed to visitors, but arrangements were by this stage formalized to encompass set opening hours on one or two days a week.

Chapter 5
The Melbourne Statues and Jan van Nost

Opposite Van Nost's figure of Mercury, thought to be based on a Renaissance original by Giambologna, provides a striking focal point on the main lawns.

Within the perfectly preserved eighteenth-century bone structure of this garden, its collection of ornaments remains another remarkably unchanged feature. Ranging from a playful set of naughty cherubs to an imposing classical figure of Mercury poised on one wing-sandalled foot, they were purchased by Thomas Coke to adorn his newly laid out gardens, and have remained there for the last 300 years.

All the statues in the garden came from the workshop of Jan van Nost, a Flemish craftsman who had arrived in England around 1679 to earn his living as a stone carver. He is thought to have started out at a junior level, helping with projects at Windsor Castle, but by the end of the century he had become a wealthy man with his own large workshop near Hyde Park in London, where he sold both traditional carved stone pieces and the more recently popular cast-lead figures to the great and good around the country.

As the fashion for formal gardens had spread during the late seventeenth century, so too did the demand for statuary, urns and vases with which to adorn them. Traditionally each of these pieces would have been individually carved by hand from a block of stone or marble in a process that was highly skilled, slow and – consequently – expensive. By the late seventeenth century, however, lead was increasingly being used to make fountains, statues and other garden ornaments. It was cheaper than carved stone or cast bronze, it was quick and relatively easy to work with and, best of all from a business perspective, the same mould could be used repeatedly to make many replica pieces.

Lead had been widely used for architectural features since at least the Middle Ages, originally in a simple form for practical items of pipework but also with increasingly decorative finishes for roofs and drain hoppers. Then, in the seventeenth century, a number of artist craftsmen began forming this highly malleable metal into purely ornamental objects, and van Nost was a skilled early adopter of this new practice.

After his journeyman work at Windsor Castle, van Nost had gone on to serve as an assistant in the London workshop of Arnold Quellin. Quellin was another Flemish craftsman, who had come to England around 1672 and in time became one of the most celebrated sculptors in the country. When Quellin died in 1686, at the age of just thirty-three, van Nost swiftly married his widow and in the process also acquired his workshop, client list and a collection of sculptural figures from which casts could be taken.

Although he had demonstrable skill with a hammer and chisel, van Nost soon chose to specialize in lead statues that, as

was the fashion of the day, were usually painted after carving, either to look like stone or with a polychrome finish that was intended to emulate the natural appearance of skin, hair and clothing. (The glorious silvery-grey patina of naturally aged lead, which today we prize so highly, only began to be appreciated relatively recently.)

There were some at the time who scoffed at this 'factory approach' to the production of artistic pieces, but van Nost's many influential patrons included the Duke of Devonshire at Chatsworth and, in due course, Queen Anne at Hampton Court. Having acquired royal patronage, van Nost's business was essentially secured as Anne's courtiers queued up to place orders of their own.

Thomas was one such enthusiastic customer, and the Melbourne Hall archives contain a whole folder of correspondence from John Nost, as he signed himself. He wrote in a clear and elegant hand that is far easier for modern readers to decipher than that of many of Thomas's correspondents, and his notes are often quite conversational in tone. The letter he wrote on 1 July 1699 to 'the Honble Thomas Coke Esqr att Melbourne in Darbyshire' is a good example. In it he writes that 'I hope you will pardon my not answering your desires sooner. I had set up 2 modles of boys but they were not to my mind'. He goes on to explain that he had been called out of town by some troublesome issues that 'hath been a great hindrance to me many Businesses But I will now with all speed Dispach you Boys with all the Care I can'.

Whether this expression of dissatisfaction with the quality of his work was genuine or just an early example of skilful client management to excuse a delay, it is clear that van Nost was as accomplished a businessman as he was a craftsman. He certainly knew when to flatter his important patrons, and when to politely draw a line.

Inevitably, many of van Nost's letters in the Melbourne Hall archive are concerned with prices and practicalities. From time to time, Thomas appears to have attempted a little bit of haggling, eliciting a response from 'Yr Hons most humble and obliged Servt John Nost', in which he firmly refuses to play ball: 'I have made as Nice a Calculation as can be & find it cannot be done under the Prises than is rated above & the lowest Prises I have set down.'

In the end, Thomas went on to purchase various sculptures, all of which he meticulously noted down in his household accounts, including '4 Pr Boyes cast in Mettall – 42-00-00' and 'Perseus & Andromeda Do – 45-00-00'. To this shopping list were added bills for cleaning and polishing, 'Wharfidge, Cartridge & Portridge'. All in all, it was an expensive exercise, but given that these figures have now enhanced the grounds of Melbourne Hall for over 300 years, it can most definitely be counted as money well spent.

Opposite The lead Cupid, spouting a slender fountain of water, and two more gambolling around their stone plinths, playfully encourage garden visitors to explore beyond the central network of paths.

Left The tussle between a pair of winged *amorini*, probably the brothers Eros and Anteros, is comically highlighted by caps of fresh snow.

Below The ordered geometry of the formal parts of the garden, including the lines of pollarded limes which radiate out from the Four Seasons Urn, is beautifully highlighted by snowfall and strong shadows.

Right The Four Seasons Urn, a gift from Queen Anne to Thomas Coke, is the finest piece of sculpture in the garden and has stood at this confluence of radiating lime avenues since he first took possession of it.

In fact, the most expensive piece in Thomas's collection was not actually purchased by him. There is a receipt in the archives showing that the Four Seasons Urn, which stands proudly at the highest point in the garden, was priced by van Nost at £100, but that hefty price tag was met by Queen Anne, who presented it as a gift to her loyal courtier.

It is an ornate piece, which stands nearly 2.5 m (8 ft) high on a stone base that is believed to have been carved by the renowned French stonemason Devigne for the price of £6. The sides of the urn are decorated with cherubs and swags of foliage, it is topped by a basket overflowing with fruit and flowers, and the whole piece is held aloft by four grinning monkeys with long and winding tails. Representations of spring, summer, autumn and winter decorate the four handles on the lid and explain how this renowned piece acquired its name.

The Four Seasons Urn has almost certainly never moved from the exact position where Thomas first instructed it to be placed, sitting at a high point in the garden where it serves both as an eye-catching focal point and a marker at the axis point of four radial avenues of lime trees. In contrast, a number of other figures have taken quite a circuitous route to their current resting places.

The plan of the garden by the surveyor Mr Kirkland, dated 1722, clearly shows that all Thomas's little cherubs were originally ranged down either side of the central path that leads from the house to the Great Basin. This rather staged presentation was a common practice in gardens at the time but at some point, probably in the early nineteenth century, they were moved into their current positions in various hedge alcoves along the path by the Great Basin, and this more discreet and playful arrangement is infinitely more appealing to modern eyes.

They may have remained in position for several hundred years, but they have gently moved in other ways over the intervening centuries. Lead is a notoriously soft metal and gravity is an inexorable force, so time has taken its toll on a number of the figures in the garden.

In van Nost's day, the manufacturing process began by taking a cast from an original sculpture, then inserting a core material (usually gypsum) and an internal iron support structure before the mould was filled with lead. This meant that if the lead surface ever became damaged and water got into the figure there was a significant risk that the iron armature would rust, causing it to expand and inflict further damage on the soft lead from the inside outwards. As a result, very few outdoor sculptures from this period have survived unscathed, since there are so many potential causes of damage, ranging from accidental impact to nibbling squirrels who, bizarrely, are inordinately fond of sharpening their teeth on pieces of lead.

The Four Seasons Urn, with its lifelike decorations of fruit, has proved particularly popular with these bushy-tailed vandals,

Opposite The receipt for this figure of Andromeda, and her partner Perseus, is still held in the Melbourne Hall archives.

Left A chubby pair of winged *amorini* in a conciliatory embrace.

Left The architectural structure of meticulously clipped yew provides a framing device for many of the statues in the garden, including this animated figure of Andromeda.

Left The figure of Perseus, triumphantly raising the severed head of Medusa, is finely framed by a niche in the yew hedge.

but it is the statue of Mercury, which stands on the lowest axis of the central path down to the Great Basin, that has most suffered with the passage of time. Given that it is the largest figurative piece in the garden, this is perhaps unsurprising, but what was not expected was the conclusion of a conservation report commissioned in 1979 by Peter Kerr, Twelfth Marquess of Lothian (father of the current owner, Ralph). This concluded that the statue of Mercury that stood in the garden was actually a slush-cast copy of the van Nost original. It is likely to have been made in the 1910s by W.J. Furse and Co. who 'restored' the figure for Sir Walter Kerr.

Slush casting is an easier and cheaper method than the solid casting process used in van Nost's sculpture yard. It involves lining a cold mould with successive thin coats of molten lead until the required thickness is achieved. Since this produces a series of layers, rather like a sheet of puff pastry, the resultant figure will be neither as strong nor as resistant to corrosion as one that has been solid cast using the traditional method.

The conservator who produced the 1979 report was Andrew Naylor from Berwickshire in Scotland, and in it he noted with some disapproval that the figure had been 'produced in an unnecessarily large number of separate piece (fourteen, plus wings and baton) which would seem to indicate that the founder was not experienced in the casting of statuary.' He was even more dismayed to discover that:

> *. . . [the] interior of the figure was partly filled with plaster of Paris and sand, and partly with approximately 50 kilos of lead which had been poured into the lower torso. Being naturally unstable, the addition of so much weight added tremendously to the stress on the bronze armature and I feel sure, was a major contributing factor in the subsequent toppling of the statue.*

His solution was to carefully dismantle, clean, patch and reassemble the figure around a stainless-steel armature. Finally, he filled the entire statue with polyurethane foam – a packing material which may very possibly prove equally distressing to conservators of the future.

It is always challenging for the custodians of historically important pieces to decide on the best course of action for their preservation, since techniques and materials are constantly being re-evaluated. Conservators who once prided themselves on being able to invisibly repair ancient ceramics now prefer to make a feature of the damaged sections, in the Japanese *kintsugi* style. Among lead conservators, there is currently some debate about the merits of recreating a painted finish on statues where fragmentary evidence of colour still remains. The cherubs at Melbourne Hall were originally painted to look like white marble and appear to have been regularly repainted over the years. In fact, there are still traces of white paint clearly visible in places, but at Melbourne Hall, for the time being at least, van Nost's figures will continue to stand in all their own, glorious unvarnished finish.

Left Jan van Nost's figure of Mercury stands, dramatically poised on one wing-sandalled foot, at the confluence of paths on the main lawns.

VIRES ACQUIRIT EUNDO
COMMEMORATIVE URN
BICENTENNIAL • INSTALLED ON
TOOK ITS NAME • ALSO TO

Melbourne, Australia

Opposite The Australian Commemorative Bicentennial Urn in lead, with crest and inscription vividly highlighted, was commissioned by Ralph's parents to commemorate the bicentenary of Australia.

Below The urn stands in a quiet spot adjoining the Dell, on ground carpeted with the pungent but pretty wild garlic (*Allium ursinum*).

Lord Melbourne, the Second Viscount Melbourne, became Prime Minister to King William IV and it was while holding this office, in 1837, that he gave his name to the Australian settlement originally known as Bearbrass or Batmania. This had been an adjunct to the primary settlement of Williamstown, which was named in honour of King William, but in time superseded and subsequently absorbed it. This connection was formally recognized in 1988 with the installation of the commemorative Melbourne Urn. This bears a smartly painted crest incorporating the motto 'Vires acquaint eundo, Virtute et Fide', which means 'Acquaint yourself with strength by going with strength and faith.' Underneath is an inscription, picked out in gold lettering:

Commemorative urn installed on September twenty fourth 1988 by Ian Haig, Agent General for Victoria, on the occasion of the Australian Bicentennial: Also to recall Queen Victoria's Prime Minister Viscount Melbourne from whom the city of Melbourne took its name

An Australian visitor to Melbourne, Derbyshire, in 1876 was dismayed to hear that the village folk had never heard of another Melbourne. Periodic attempts have been made to forge lasting links between the two Melbournes, but they are so far removed from one another in space, size and culture that these have had limited success.

Chapter 6
Water and the Work of George Sorocold

Opposite The Fountain Walk is a creative *tour de force* but also a magnificent example of hydraulic engineering in practice, producing three perfectly matched columns of water that sparkle and dance in this calm green section of the garden.

Water is at the heart of the Melbourne Hall gardens. The Great Basin is the most obvious example – a mirror-like focal point for the great vista that leads out from the house, and a perfect reflective foil for the Birdcage that is set close to its farther bank – but there is also a series of three serene little fountains set along the green and shady Fountain Walk, two more frame the outer edges of the central parterre, and the vast expanse of the Pool lies just beyond the garden walls.

The very name of this place emphasizes the importance of water to Melbourne's existence. A stream, or 'bourne', runs into the Pool, and the Pool itself was engineered to feed a small mill, or 'mel'. (In recent years the mill building was converted into a private house, but the Domesday Book of 1086 mentions a mill standing on approximately the same site.) There is also an unsubstantiated but highly plausible theory that in its earliest times the Hall and garden may have been fully moated. This was common practice for medieval manor houses of the twelfth and thirteenth centuries and was also a regular feature of bishop's palaces. For example, the Bishop of Coventry and Lichfield had a moated palace at Eccleshall Castle, only 80 km (50 miles) from Melbourne, and the whole cathedral close at nearby Lichfield was moated. Since Melbourne Hall was also a bishop's palace before Sir John Coke acquired the lease, a former moat would not be surprising.

Whatever the detail, we know that there has always been water within the gardens at Melbourne Hall. For hundreds of years this took the very practical form of stew ponds that were kept stocked with fish conveniently ready to be caught for the kitchen. Early plans show these fish ponds on the site that today is occupied by the lower four quarter lawns on the east side of the house, but in 1699 Thomas issued an instruction to 'level the Islands within the motes' and create 'two fountains slop'd with green turf'.

At a time when water features were increasingly fashionable and Thomas was actively expanding his gardens, he appears to have decided that what he already had was not quite good enough. He dreamed of a grand avenue linking three separate ponds, or 'basins', each with a fountain and each cut into a different shape – one like the sun, one like the moon and one with four small star-like points that is said to have been inspired by the famous Apollo fountain at Versailles.

He also planned for a fountain at the end of what would come to be called the Library Walk, and a partner fountain at the end of the Yew Tunnel. Then, last but by no means least, he wanted to sweep away the modified remains of his grandfather's stew ponds,

Left Where there is water there will be water fowl, and swans regularly visit the Great Basin within the gardens of Melbourne Hall and, shown here, the Pool just outside its perimeter.

Opposite Ever since its height and flow were regulated by hydraulic engineer George Sorocold, the Pool has been a popular destination for the people of Melbourne.

to create a Great Basin further east, giving a gracious focus to his garden.

The fashion in that time of formal garden design was for large rectangular pools, and the longer the better. Perhaps the most notable example of this style is the Long Water at Hampton Court, created under the instruction of King Charles II in 1660, very shortly after his restoration to the throne. As a court regular, this magnificent canal would certainly have been well known to Thomas.

Unfortunately (or fortunately, depending on your point of view), the lie of the land at Melbourne Hall thwarted any temptation towards overambitious excavation. Immediately outside the end wall of the garden a fast-flowing stream known as Carr Brook runs across the entire site, and beyond it the land rises steeply away. Faced with this irritating lack of flat land, Thomas appears to have decided to simply make his own pool as large as he reasonably could.

So it was that in 1704 the two old ponds on the lower lawns were filled in using the spoil generated by the excavation of the Great Basin. The shape that Thomas specified for his new pool is yet another example of his clever eye for design. On the house side it was fashionably rectilinear, with clearly defined right-angled corners, but on the far side it curved out to almost touch the end wall. The resulting elliptical shape is one that plays with perspective and tricks the eye into believing that the water occupies a much larger space than it does in reality. The flat front bank initially included a semi-circular apron of land that pushed out into the water. There is no known record of exactly when this was removed, but it may well have occurred in the early nineteenth century when the water level in the basin was raised. Aside from this minor modification, the Great Basin has remained otherwise unchanged ever since.

In contrast to the meticulously designed Great Basin, the 8-hectare (20-acre) Pool – which sits just outside the main garden boundaries and today is a well-known local beauty spot popular with the dog-walking fraternity – appears untouched by either the hand of man or the passage of time. The reality is rather different, on both counts.

Shortly after the Norman Conquest there was already a mill there, as mentioned in the Domesday Book, and by Thomas's day it was served by the present Pool. The Melbourne Hall estate finally acquired ownership of the mill and the Pool in 1789, having previously leased them from the Hastings family of Donington Hall since 1701. Today the Old Mill still forms part of the Melbourne Hall estate, and is currently home to the estate manager, but it was operating as a working mill until as recently as 1968, nearly 900 years after the earliest record of such activity on the site.

Despite his interest in the mill, Thomas was very much in two minds about the desirability of having the Pool so close to

Left In autumn, the ornamental impact of seasonal leaf colour is multiplied magnificently in the mirror-like surface of the Great Basin.

Above Viewed from the banks of the Great Basin, its cleverly elliptical shape tricks the eye into perceiving it as a larger body of water than it really is.

Right Swans are known to mate for life, and a devoted pair which lived on the Great Basin for many years were very popular with visitors.

Opposite The lovely nodding pond cypress (*Taxodium distichum* var. *imbricarium* 'Nutans') grows best with its roots close to water, and thrives on the banks of the Great Basin.

Left In the very early mornings, mist frequently rises from the surface of the Great Basin, lending a touch of fairy-tale magic to the scene.

Above The Sun Pool is tucked away on the Fountain Walk, where its surface shimmers in the cool green setting.

Right Each slender fountain animates the scene, rising in a crystalline column then falling with a musical tinkle to send out rippling circles on the surface of the pool.

Opposite The fountains are aligned with the interconnecting network of paths, so that each one can be viewed from many different aspects.

his property. At that time the body of water was larger than it is now and was not always picturesque. The water level would rise and fall as it was drawn off to power the mill, exposing mud in the process, and one section of the perimeter was used as a horse wash by the townsfolk of Melbourne. In addition, local women came to launder clothes at a powerful spring that fed into the Pool at a site near the church that was known as the 'washing well'.

All in all, Thomas decided the Pool was more trouble than it was worth. It was, he declared so 'noisome and unhealthy' to his household that he was going to make arrangements to have it completely drained as soon as he could lease it from the Hastings estate. Perhaps he had in mind Francis Bacon's old essay of eighty years earlier, in which he wrote that 'fountains . . . are a great beauty and refreshment; but pools mar all, and make the garden unwholesome, and full of flies and frogs.' However, by 1706 an ingenious local hydraulic engineer called George Sorocold had made him think differently.

Not much is known about Sorocold's early years beyond the fact that he was born in Derby around 1668, but by the time of his death he was widely renowned as a pioneer in the field of hydraulic engineering. He had installed the first piped water supply in Derby in 1692, designed a water wheel to power the machinery at the Derby Silk Mill and, in later life, became a notable national figure. He went on to work as far afield as London, where his projects included devising a novel style of water wheel under the old London Bridge, while finding time to father no fewer than thirteen children, of whom eight survived.

Sorocold swiftly talked Thomas out of any thoughts of draining the pool. Instead, he recommended raising the surface of the water until it sat permanently at 60 cm (24 in) above its former level. This, he demonstrated, would produce sufficient water pressure to power all the fountains that Thomas desired.

To this end a network of pipes was laid around the garden, some of which were made from elm, a strong and remarkably rot-resistant wood that for centuries had been widely used both for coffins and to carry water. This also proved to be an excellent choice. Estate records show that work on the majority of the water features was completed between 1704 and 1706, but when one of the fountains sprang a leak in 2020 the problem was eventually traced back to a section of one of those original elm pipes that, after 300 years, had finally succumbed to old age. (Even then, most of the ancient pipe was found to be sufficiently sound, so only the damaged section was repaired, using clay, to avoid unnecessary disruption to the wider gardens.)

The pipes were linked to feed each of the five fountains in the garden, which sent up crystalline spouts of water that sparkled elegantly against the predominantly green backdrop. The new fountains were an instant hit with everyone except for the unfortunate vicar, who was more than a little annoyed to

Right Ancient yew hedges, youthful swamp cypresses (*Taxodium distichum*) and sword-like clumps of flag iris frame the timeless beauty of Robert Bakewell's gilded Birdcage.

discover that his beloved orchard had been flooded in the process of raising the water level of the Pool.

Sorocold wrote to update Thomas on his successful handling of this tricky situation in 1706. 'I visited the Parson yesterday who seemed a little uneased about the lower end of his Orchard being under water but upon taking a Pott or two & faire promises to fill up that part with all speed, he begun your health in a Bumper!' After Sorocold had made the necessary adjustments the system worked perfectly, the fountains could be balanced so that each plume of water was at the same height as all the others, and today, 300 years later, that same system continues to power the spouts.

The classic French text on garden design by Dézallier d'Argenville, which was translated into English as *The Theory and Practice of Gardening* by John James of Greenwich in 1712, perfectly expresses the enduring attraction of such water features. Fountains, he wrote:

> *. . . seem to animate [the garden], by the murmuring and spouting of their Waters, and produce those admirable Beauties, that the Eye is scarce ever satisfied with beholding them . . . Fountains and water-Works are the Life of a Garden; 'tis these make the principal Ornament of it, and which animate and invigorate it, and, if I may so say, give it new Life and Spirit. 'Tis certain, that a Garden, be it in other respects never so fine, if it want Water, appears dull and melancholy, and is deficient in one of its greatest Beauties.*

James also offered very specific advice on how these water features might best be used in a garden design:

> *The Fountains [should] be disposed in such manner, that they may be seen almost all at a time, and that the Water-Spouts may range and aline one with another, which is the Beauty of them: This Repetition makes a Confusion very agreeable to the Eye, which supposes them to be more in Number that they really are . . . [and] when you can have them in Groves, 'tis a double Satisfaction; Water there being, as it were, in its Center; besides, the Verdure of the Trees serves as a Ground to set it off, and improves the very Whiteness of the Water; the Purling and Murmur of it strikes the Ear too the more agreeably, by the Stilness and Echo that reigns in the Woods.*

John James could well have been describing the three elegant spouts of water that today still punctuate the Fountain Walk in precisely this manner.

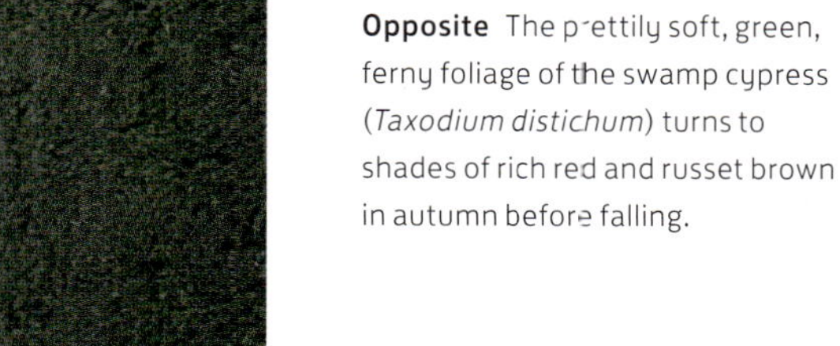

Opposite The prettily soft, green, ferny foliage of the swamp cypress (*Taxodium distichum*) turns to shades of rich red and russet brown in autumn before falling.

Left Running down the garden from the Muniment Room, the Library Walk ends at a stone-edged pond with a playful *putti* fountain at its centre.

Overleaf Mature trees, carefully maintained hedges, and a variety of water features form the enduring heart of the garden.

Left The avenues of lime trees are pollarded every three years, as they have been for centuries, although the job has become easier in recent years with the advent of the cherry picker.

Below The cherry picker has also revolutionized the hedge-cutting process, making it quicker and a great deal safer than the days when staff would simply rest their ladders against the surface of the yew.

Opposite It may take less muscle to operate an electric hedge cutter than traditional manual shears, but an expert eye is still essential to produce a professional finish.

Estate Maintenance

The lime avenues are pollarded every three years, although the hedges formed by the low twiggy growth (which these trees naturally throw out from their trunks) are cut annually. Full pollarding is a major undertaking for the estate team, and it is usually the first job they tackle after their restorative Christmas break. In total, there are 182 limes in need of a haircut and it takes two people at least six weeks to attend to them all, working off cherry pickers and hydraulic platforms, using saws and small hatchets to cut every branch tight back to its main structure. Thankfully, the low hedges are a less daunting prospect. These are tackled with mechanical hedge cutters in August, when there are certain to be no birds nesting in the branches.

Cutting the hundreds of metres of yew hedges around the garden is the biggest annual job of all. Work generally begins as soon as the garden closes to visitors at the end of August and can go on until almost Christmas. Once upon a time, the men used to just lean a ladder up against the surface of whichever hedge they were working on, leaning out to cut from side to side. They accessed the top of the Yew Tunnel by working methodically from within it, sticking a ladder vertically up the middle and pushing through until their head and shoulders emerged on the upper side. These days, hydraulic platforms make this job a great deal safer and more efficient, but it is still a massive undertaking.

Paths are another enormous maintenance issue, albeit one that most visitors take completely for granted. These are surfaced with Golden Amber self-binding gravel from the Breedon Quarry (the same mix as is used at Buckingham Palace). Metal edges have been installed along many of the paths to help keep them neat and contained. Elsewhere, drainage has been an ongoing issue. In the archives, bills for drainage work, dated 1844, show that Lord Melbourne was conscious of the problem. His work was continued by Lord Walter Kerr, who spent heavily on this essential element between 1905 and 1920. And it still goes on to the present day. On the Library Walk, for example, heavy rainfall repeatedly washed the gravel surface downhill and into the cherub pools, until about twenty years ago when land drains were installed with great trouble and expense.

Other maintenance issues are, thankfully, more once-in-a-lifetime challenges. The islands in the Pool, which were created and planted by William Pontey in the mid-nineteenth century, had become extremely overgrown by 2012, when Marie-Claire directed that they be restored. This was a huge logistical challenge, involving the removal of about sixty trees. Even gaining access to the islands was no simple matter. Planning and preparation took almost two years, during which time the estate manager, Ian Earl, devised a raft kept afloat by forty oil drums on which a tractor could be transported across the Pool. The work took three months in all, during which time the estate team rowed over to the islands every day, accompanied by the assistant's two Labradors, which faithfully swam alongside the boat to keep them company.

Chapter 7
Wrought Iron and Robert Bakewell

Opposite Since it was installed in 1708, Robert Bakewell's Birdcage has been the crowning glory of the gardens at Melbourne Hall.

The elegant Birdcage which sits on the far side of the Great Basin, is one of the defining features of Melbourne Hall gardens. With its extraordinarily ornate wrought ironwork highlighted with gilded details that glint whenever the light catches them, it has served as the key focal point in the gardens since 1708.

When Thomas Coke commissioned this jewel box of a structure to stand sentinel behind his newly formed Great Basin, he would have been inspired by many similar decorative structures that he doubtless saw in other great gardens, both here and abroad. Treillage, as it was generally called at this time, had been a feature of the smarter sort of gardens since the Medieval age, when timber was used to create shade and privacy by providing a supportive framework for climbing plants. As the years passed these practical frames had become increasingly ornate and by the turn of the eighteenth century, when Thomas was developing his plans for Melbourne Hall, they were being treated as decorative objects in their own right.

There was one significant problem. Since the structures were made of wood, they needed regular maintenance to protect them from collapse. The issue was addressed in the seminal French work *La Théorie et la Practique du Jardinage* by Dézallier d'Argenville (published in Paris in 1709 and translated into English by John James in 1712). In it he wrote:

> *Tis not so much the Fashion at present, to make Porticos, Arbors, and Cabinets of Lattice-work, in Gardens, yet they ought still to be made in some Places; and 'tis certain, these Pieces of Architecture, well disposed, have something in them very beautiful and magnificent; they raise and improve the natural Beauty of Gardens extremely; but as they are very chargeable to make and keep up, and continually liable to decay, most People are out of Conceit with them.*

In fact, he also commented, features of this sort 'demand a Royal Purse, and are to be undertaken only by Princes, Ministers of State, and Persons of the highest Quality.'

The book contains a number of engravings illustrating a range of patterns from the relatively simple to the distinctly palatial, and in essential style and effect they are very reminiscent of the Birdcage. Since Thomas is among a great number of lords, earls and other nobles who are listed as being subscribers to the English translation, this is unlikely to be a coincidence.

There is no clear evidence to suggest how Thomas came up with the idea to make his Birdcage out of wrought iron rather than short-lived timber, but we do know that this was a time

Left Illustrations of *Treillage* were included in many gardening books, such as this detailed gateway drawn by Alexandre Le Blonde, which featured in a 1722 edition of *La Théorie et la Pratique du Jardinage*.

Opposite In the estate archives, a statement of account from Robert Bakewell to Elizabeth (Betsy) Coke, dated 1709, shows his handwriting to have been as ornamental as his ironwork.

when wrought ironwork was becoming increasingly popular and elaborate, and nowhere more so than in the royal court where he was a regular presence.

The new trend had gained momentum since the 1689 coronation of William and Mary, who were both keen garden enthusiasts and great admirers of the wrought ironwork of master craftsman Jean Tijou. He was a Huguenot refugee from the Netherlands, and there is no record of exactly when he arrived in this country, but by the time of the coronation Tijou had begun transforming the quality of English decorative ironwork with a level of elaborate artistry that had never been seen before. Most notable among his many British works was the set of intricate riverside gates that Tijou made at Hampton Court Palace. Those gates are still extremely impressive today, but to Thomas and his contemporaries they must have looked absolutely extraordinary.

Basic wrought ironwork had been around for many hundreds of years. Making it was a heavy, rough and dirty business in which white-hot raw pig iron was repeatedly lifted, bent and beaten with a hammer to produce a material that was highly malleable. This could be shaped into a wide range of objects, but in the hands of a skilled craftsman like Tijou, the process was elevated to an artform. Writing in 1957, the blacksmith Raymond Lister became quite poetic in his appreciation of the medium:

> *Iron that has been heated and beaten into shape at the anvil by a sensitive blacksmith seems to grow, to be alive. Sinuous arms thread their way like tendrils through labyrinthine panels, terminating in scrolls that seem to whirl around like nebulae; straight bars twist themselves upwards screw-like to soar into rows of miniature spires, each winged like a bird; the variety is endless. It is as if an abstract ballet had been solidified for all to enjoy for all time.*

Tijou's work was highly ornamented, and he had a particular fondness for the sheet-metal adornments known as repoussé work, which he used to make acanthus leaves, flowers and other decorations including masks.

Thanks to his royal patronage and the quality of his work, Tijou was much in demand and could command the highest fees. However, to realize his elaborate designs, he needed an army of other smiths and apprentices, and it is thought that a young lad called Robert Bakewell was one of the many who worked on Tijou's landmark pieces.

Bakewell was born in Uttoxeter, Staffordshire, in 1682 into a family of smiths and was only fourteen when his father died. There are no solid documentary records, but it is most likely that the boy had always intended to follow in his father's footsteps and, when his widowed mother quickly married another smith working in the area, Robert was sent to London to take up an

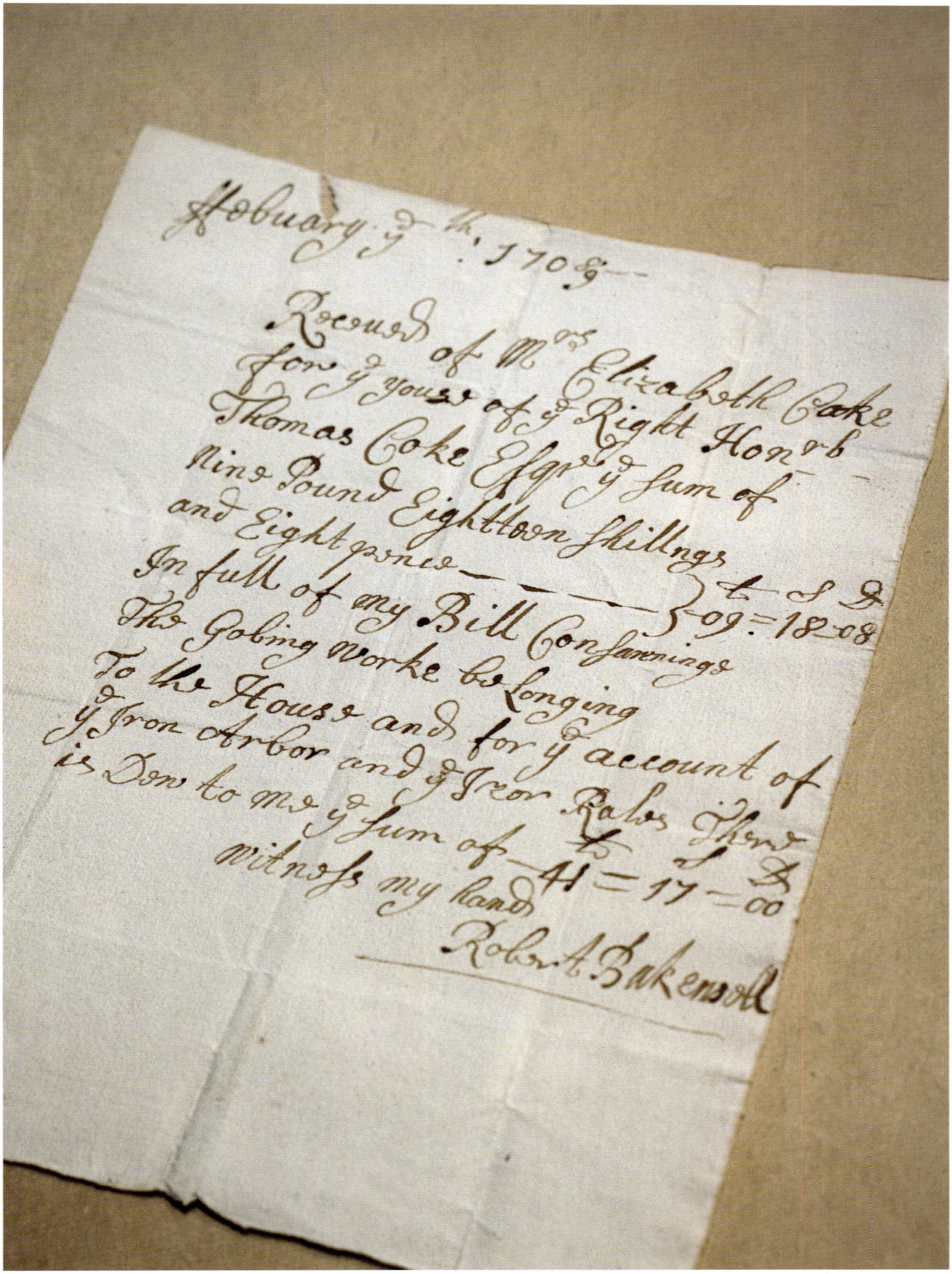

Febuary ye 7th: 1708/9 ——

Receved of Mrs Elizabeth Coke
for ye use of ye Right Honrble
Thomas Coke Esqr ye sum of
Nine Pound Eightteen Shillings
and Eight pence ———— } £ S D
09 = 18 = 08
In full of my Bill Consarnings
The Gobing worke belonging
To the House and for ye account of
ye Iron Arbor and ye Iron Rales there
is Don to me ye sum of £ S D
41 = 17 = 00
witness my hand

Robert Bakewell

apprenticeship with one of the smiths who is known to have been working on Tijou's designs at Hampton Court.

There is a similar lack of evidence as to how Bakewell came to the attention of Thomas Coke but, given that they would both have spent a lot of time at Hampton Court, it is perhaps not surprising that their paths crossed eventually. It is also no surprise that Thomas would have preferred to scout for affordable new talent rather than paying above the odds for an overbooked celebrity craftsman.

Whatever the precise sequence of events leading up to that point, we know that in 1706 Robert Bakewell arrived in Melbourne. He was twenty-five years old, and the Birdcage appears to have been his first significant independent commission. There is a record of him having made some railings for Thomas's London house, in St James's Place, for which he was paid £18 7s 3d in June 1706 but, since he was almost certainly based in Melbourne by this time, the railings may well have been a sort of trial piece as the two men made plans and preparations for the main event.

In total, Bakewell spent five years working at Melbourne Hall and the Birdcage is still today regarded as his virtuoso piece. As twentieth-century blacksmith Raymond Lister observed in his book *Decorative Wrought Ironwork in Great Britain*, 'All the Tijou trappings are there – masks, acanthus leaves, swags, cloths of estate, and an abundance of robust scrollwork. But it is all more tasteful, it is restrained in comparison with the eruptive leafage of Tijou's Hampton Court screens.'

Writing from the perspective of a professional in the craft, Lister went on to say:

> *. . . when we come to the underlying structure and to the magnificent scrollwork, here is indeed a different aspect of Bakewell's work. For in that he is the equal at least of Tijou. He even, within the discipline, the almost classical style of his work, seems to capture something of the urgency of the pure forged work of early smiths . . . To stand within the arbour and look upwards, to see those naturalistic tendrils and leaves creeping down and threading their way along the bars of the dome is to experience [how the] smith in the joy of creation has transcended his medium and sought to emulate nature herself.*

Right The intricate dome of the Birdcage, overlaid with sinuous tendrils and delicately naturalistic foliage, was a sensational achievement in Bakewell's day, and still has the power to amaze and delight visitors today.

Left Frosted with a covering of snow, the elegant scrollwork and delicately trailing strands of various plants, form an impressive sight.

Although Bakewell's work is marked by a certain refined elevation, the man himself appears to have been considerably more down to earth, and he certainly didn't spend all his time working. His forge was set up in the basement of the building known today as Stone House, an attractive private home in a quiet corner of Melbourne next to the church. At the turn of the eighteenth century, however, it appears to have been a rather rowdy establishment. The upper floors were occupied by Elizabeth Fisher and her five daughters, a seemingly feisty bunch who had such a tempestuous family dynamic that their mother made specific mention in her will about how the living space was to be divided up after her death if the girls couldn't get on.

One of those girls, also called Elizabeth, was clearly more favourably inclined towards Robert than she was towards her siblings. The parish register for 26 October 1709 records the baptism of 'Bakewell Fisher ye bastard child of Robert Bakewell and Elizabeth Fisher' but, although he continued to live in Melbourne for another two years, at no point did he decide to marry the mother of his first-born child.

Perhaps it is no surprise that by 3 March 1711, Betsy Coke was keen to see the back of Robert. On that day she wrote to Thomas to say that 'I hasten Mr Bakewell with the finishing of your work, for his behaviour is not to be borne with in respect to this place, but I will not be tedious in particulars.'

Bakewell may have been a bit of a scoundrel, but he appears to have been charming with it. Even though Betsy sincerely wished to be rid of him, she was not prepared to turf him out, although she would have been well within her rights to do so on Thomas's behalf. Instead, in early April 1711 she wrote to Thomas about Bakewell once again, saying that:

> *. . . he has got a shop fitting up at Derby but is so miserable poor that I believe he can't remove til he has some money, so far as five pounds I have promised to let him have till I hear from you, to leave him without excuse in going. He has sent home a very noble piece for my Lord Gore and is further engaged in work for my Lord Chesterfield and my Lord Ferrers has lately sent to him also, so I have been unwilling to press his goeing to expose him too much since his livelihood depends upon it.*

She also noted that 'Mr Bakewell has finished your work of the Arbour, and has not brought in any account of it, but says, when you have seen it, he will refer himself to you'.

Bakewell received £120 for making the main structure, and an additional £6 when he returned two years later to add the cupola, noted in the estate records as 'A turret for the top of the Iron Arbour'. Like many a craftsperson down the ages, the inexperienced Bakewell, desperately keen to secure his first big commission, appears to have significantly underestimated the time and expense that would be entailed in producing the Birdcage.

Opposite The 'smalt blue' and gilded finish of the Birdcage today is very close to the appearance it would have had in Thomas Coke's day, and is an important defence against the corrosive power of the elements.

Left Since Marie-Claire reopened an avenue between the trees on the rising land behind the garden, the impact of this main axis has been considerably enhanced.

Overleaf In sunshine or in silhouette, Robert Bakewell's Birdcage is one of the great glories of the gardens at Melbourne Hall.

His problems may well have been compounded by the prevailing convention of that time by which ironwork was paid for according to its weight, not just its size and design, which meant that a complicated piece could easily become an economic liability for its creator. It was in this context that Betsy wrote again to her brother saying 'he says you should tell him how much you will pay when you see what he has made'.

After leaving Melbourne, Bakewell's fortunes did recover and he went on to produce many other widely celebrated pieces, including the chancel screen and gates in the Church of All Saints (now the cathedral) at Derby. He made these between 1722 and 1725 for the sum of £338 10s 9d, demonstrating that, by this stage, he had learned an important lesson about realistically pricing a job.

Bakewell returned to Melbourne Hall at least once more, in 1725, when he made the lyre-shaped balustrading that marks the south end of the terrace, where it overlooks the Pool. We know he also produced many pieces for the gardens of other grand patrons, but today most surviving pieces of Bakewell's work (and those of his contemporaries) are connected with ecclesiastical and other public buildings. This is largely thanks to the craze for Capability Brown landscapes of faux-natural parkland, which swept away so many formal gardens just a few decades after Bakewell finished ornamenting them, but it is also due to a natural phenomenon.

Rust is a huge threat to wrought ironwork, quick to take hold and aggressive in its destructive progress. Proper maintenance is essential to prevent it from causing significant damage, and many fine pieces have been lost for want of a coat of paint, but the Birdcage has benefitted from regular care throughout its long existence.

In a sense, even the choice of paint colour is a significant act of ongoing conservation. Today we tend to think of black as the standard colour with which to paint railings and other ironwork, but this was scarcely used until 1861 when the nation joined Queen Victoria in mourning the death of her beloved Prince Albert. In the eighteenth century 'smalt blue' (made from powdered cobalt glass) and gold leaf was a popular combination for those who could afford such expensive materials. It is thought that the Melbourne Hall Birdcage was originally painted green.

Photographs of the gardens taken in the mid-nineteenth century, when Lord Palmerstone came to visit, and that capture him standing in front of the Birdcage, suggest that at that time the structure was painted pure white.

Today the Birdcage is fully restored to glory, with carefully maintained paintwork that produces an effect very similar to the fashionable eighteenth-century 'smalt blue' and gold leaf livery, and an anchoring exedra of yews that provides a deep-green backdrop that shows off every elaborate scroll and gilded leaf of this remarkable structure.

Thomas Cook, the Melbourne Travel Agent

Thomas Cook, the eponymous travel-agency entrepreneur, was born into a humble Melbourne family in 1808 and lived in the town until he was twenty. At the age of ten he started working for a market gardener, and in his later youth was apprenticed to a wood turner in the town, during which period he may have worked on replacements of the gilded wooden finials on the Birdcage. But Cook was a hard-working boy with a strong social conscience who was determined to improve not only his own lot, but that of others as well.

In 1828 he became a Baptist missionary and passionate advocate for the temperance movement, believing that men would not waste their money in the public houses if they had more wholesome activities to distract them. It was with this in mind that, on 5 July 1841, he arranged an excursion for a group of temperance supporters in Leicester to attend a rally in Loughborough. The outing was a great success, and became the foundation on which he built his 'package holiday' business.

Cook became an extremely wealthy man and based his company activities in London, but he retained a great affection for his hometown. In 1874 he tried to acquire the lease of Melbourne Hall, when the long-standing tenant Mrs Gooch passed away. Frederick Fox, the Melbourne estate agent, was taken aback by the idea of someone from such lowly origins living at the Hall, and even more horrified when he discovered that Cook intended to turn it into a grand tourist attraction. Fox took swift and decisive steps to thwart his application, but Cook did not give up on his connections with Melbourne.

In 1889, while accompanying two American visitors on a visit to the town, he was appalled to discover how many residents were still living in extremely poor conditions. Cook took direct action, paying for the construction of fourteen attractive memorial cottages and a public mission hall. Ever the practical man of business, at the same time he set up a charitable trust to rent out the houses at a rate of one penny per person per week. Today those cottages are still an attractive feature on the High Street, and continue to be owned and operated by Cook's charitable Trust – although the rent has gone up a little in the past century or so.

Opposite Robert Bakewell was also responsible for the lyre-shaped balustrading that stands at one end of the upper terrace, from where there are uninterrupted views out over the Pool.

Above Tourist pioneer Thomas Cook (1808–92) was born in poverty in Melbourne and, despite going on to make a fortune, was never considered genteel enough to take up the tenancy of Melbourne Hall.

Chapter 8
The Later Years

Opposite After the death of Thomas Coke, his ancestors did not live at Melbourne Hall for several centuries, and the garden was left in the hands of a series of tenants.

Thomas Coke died in 1727, but his garden continued, a living entity in need of constant maintenance and care. In the archive is an undated note making arrangements for the ongoing upkeep of the gardens immediately following his demise.

The proposals of John Sands of Derby Gardener, To Jno Coke & John Harding Esqrs for keeping the Gardens at Melbourne are as follow Vizt. That the said John Sands will keep all the Garden from the House to the Iron Arbour in good order, and all the Wall Trees regularly prun'd in Season, & in good order in all the Gardens, & keep all the Hedges in all the Gardens well Clipt, in their proper seasons, and keep the out Walks Mowed, as he the said John Sands shall think proper, so that they may be brought into good order by Sowing of Seeds when requir'd, and will keep all the Nurserys belonging to the late Vice Chamberlain Clear and pruned in proper season, & likewise will lay into the Gardens 60 Cart Load of good Dung every Year, with Lime and soyl, to mix with the said Dung as shall be thought most fit and Convenient either for the Good and Improvement of the Wall Trees or Kitchin Garden, All of which He the said John Sands doth agree to do, for the sum of Fifty pounds a year, and all the profits of all the said Gardens and Nurserys, and a Room and Bed for himself and Boy to Lodge in.

The practical day-to-day care of the gardens had always been left in the hands of the staff but, until this point, the successive owners of the house had taken at least some creative interest in their development. When Thomas died, so did that all important sense of proprietorial concern and, with it, any urge to expend time and money on making major changes.

Just a few years later the prevailing fashion shifted away from formal design to the deceptively simple evocations of an idealized English landscape created by Capability Brown, and almost every fine garden in the country was gradually remodelled to replace geometric terraces, paths and lawns with rolling turf, sinuous lakes and naturalistic clumps of trees. The natural topography at Melbourne Hall could, in fact, have lent itself extremely well to this treatment but, thanks to the benign indifference of subsequent owners, the perfect formality of the established garden was left intact.

Thomas's son, George Lewis Coke (1715–50), inherited the Hall from his father, but he did not come of age until 1736 and died in 1750 without producing an heir; he was therefore the last of the Cokes to live at Melbourne Hall. The estate then passed via George's sister, Charlotte, to her husband, Sir Matthew Lamb (1705–68), a lawyer who had been involved with the Melbourne estate in a professional capacity for a decade or so before he married into the family in 1740. Lamb had inherited an enormous amount of money from his uncle, some of which he had used to buy the fine Brocket Hall estate in Hertfordshire, so, when George

died, Sir Matthew chose Brocket Hall over Melbourne Hall as his family's primary residence.

Matthew died in 1768 and his son Peniston Lamb, First Viscount Melbourne (1740–1828), seems to have had equally little interest in the Melbourne estate, despite taking its name when he was made a lord in 1770. Meanwhile, his wife, Elizabeth Milbanke, devoted her own energies to reinforcing her place in the upper echelons of society through a series of advantageous romantic liaisons. It was widely believed that several of her seven children were not actually sired by her husband, including one reputed to be the son of the Prince of Wales, later George IV.

Only their first-born son, also called Peniston, was definitively legitimate but, since he predeceased his father in 1828, the family titles and estates were handed down to William Lamb, Second Viscount Melbourne (1779–1848), who would go on to become Queen Victoria's first Prime Minister, advisor and close confidant. In 1837 the city of Melbourne in Australia was named in his honour, but he was equally notable in his own lifetime for the behaviour of his wife, Lady Caroline, née Ponsonby. She was an eccentric individual with little regard for social conventions who had a widely publicized affair with Lord Byron and, when he broke off their relationship, famously denounced him as 'mad, bad and dangerous to know'.

William had also chosen Brocket Hall as his primary residence, but Melbourne Hall was for a time occupied by William's younger brother George and his wife, and Lady Caroline was sent to stay with them for a while in an attempt to keep her out of the public spotlight. There is no record of her thoughts on the gardens. Instead, she seems to have favoured the surrounding lanes, where she was observed wandering aimlessly, dressed in inappropriate footwear and feathers.

George, in contrast, lived a quieter life and spent time organizing the family archives and writing plays and poetry. It was he who created the current library at Melbourne Hall, in 1831, and it seems quite likely that he was also responsible for adding one more water feature to the gardens. The Grotto, also known as the Wishing Well, is tucked away at the far end of the Millstream Borders, in the shade of a handkerchief tree (*Davidia involucrata*). We know it did not exist in Thomas Coke's day, but there is no firm record of who did make this charming little feature. It is formed of a double-brick arch faced with tufa that is fixed in place with iron cramps, and it was given a Grade II listing in 1967. Within this arch is a low alcove containing a semi-circular marble niche, a small stone pool and the marble inscription of a poem written by George Lamb:

Rest weary stranger in this shady cave,
And taste, if languid, of the mineral wave,
There's virtue in the draught, for health that flies,

From crowded cities and their smoky skies,
Here lends her power from every glade and hill
Strength to the breeze
G. Lamb

Since the grotto is mentioned in estate records of the early 1830s, it seems reasonable to deduce that George was responsible for its creation. He also installed the cast-iron flower baskets on the upper lawns in 1834, and a year later directed the construction of a new boat house on the banks of the Pool; but in general, the maintenance of the ornamental gardens was left in the hands of the staff. By all accounts, they did a good job.

When Lord Melbourne resigned permanently from political life in 1841, he sought a change of scene at Melbourne Hall, and sent instructions to his agent Frederick Fox to stock up on port, sherry and linens ahead of his arrival in late November. He was joined at the Hall by his sister Emily and her husband Lord Palmerston (who would go on to be another of Queen Victoria's Prime Ministers). On 3 December 1841, Emily wrote that she had 'visited Melbourne. The gardens beautiful seen under the worst circumstances (under umbrellas) and it is altogether such a very comfortable place.'

Lord Melbourne did not spend a huge amount of time at Melbourne Hall, but we know that he was there in 1843 when a ball he had arranged for the servants was disrupted by a

Opposite George Lamb lived at Melbourne Hall in the early nineteenth century, but he was more interested in writing poems and plays than he was in gardening. In 1831 he created the current Library.

Below The Melbourne Hall gardens as painted by George Samuel Elgood in the later nineteenth century are remarkably close in appearance to the gardens today.

brief social insurrection. Not only the local newspapers but London publications as well, reported that the housekeeper and other senior staff had refused to dance with the lower order of servant, 'Because we consider we should lose caste, destroy the "balance of power" and break down that "conspicuous line of demarcation" that separates the housekeeper's room from the servants' hall' and 'the effluvia of grooms and coachmen reeking from the stables'. Just as matters were threatening to get seriously out of control, Lord Melbourne appeared below stairs and, 'in the most bland and affable manner, took the hand of the under housemaid, and opened the ball in a style that won all hearts.'

Lord Melbourne was at the Hall often enough to seriously consider changes and improvements there. Part of the house underwent extensive repair and improvement, and he had an ice house built in the gardens. He made a pedestrian connection into the adjoining parkland via a new bridge behind the Birdcage and had a leisure drive laid out around the Park, within a new avenue of trees called the Park Drive.

He also made himself popular locally by remodelling the Pool, which had been largely ignored since George Sorocold first modified it to power Thomas Coke's fountains over one hundred years earlier. By Lord Melbourne's tenure it had silted up and was in a sorry state. He made a retirement project of its improvement, engaging an engineer called James Davidson and a landscape gardener called William Pontey to realize his vision.

William Pontey came from a notable family of Yorkshire nurserymen, and in 1800 had written a book, entitled *Pontey's Profitable Planter*, on the planting and management of trees for 'shelter and ornament'. He also laid out a number of significant gardens in the northern counties and worked for the Dukes of Bedford at Woburn Abbey.

Remodelling the Pool was a huge project, occupying Pontey from around 1845 to 1847. In this time, he oversaw the creation of two islands within this large body of water in 1845, and their subsequent planting with trees. The newly planted islands, complemented by a new break in the woods on the far side, effectively reorganized the tree cover into bold clumps with a decidedly pastoral character. Meanwhile the wood fringing the pool was landscaped as a public park, with rustic benches and a little shell grotto called the Frog's Mouth.

It was probably also Pontey who suggested moving the weir into its present position close to the road. Here he designed a curved breast wall for additional strength and set stones into its surface in a pattern designed to make the water produce a pleasant tinkling noise that could be enjoyed by those inside the garden.

Pontey also seems to have proposed some changes within the garden itself, judging by a plan he prepared in 1846 to introduce new beds of 'American Plants' into the area near the Grotto. There is no concrete evidence that these were ever realized, but the last letter that Lord Melbourne ever wrote to his Melbourne

Opposite Tucked away at the end of the Millstream Borders lies the Grotto – fringed by epimediums and ferns – which is thought to have been the one addition that George Lamb made to the gardens during the time that he lived at Melbourne Hall.

Right The arched structure is actually made of bricks, but a dressing of tufa rocks gives it a rusticated appearance. Next to the small pool at its heart is a plaque inscribed with a verse written by George Lamb.

Right The woodland grove around the Grotto has a character quite unlike the rest of the gardens and is well worth seeking out, although visitors often miss its quiet delights in pursuit of more well-known views.

agent, just before his death in 1848, concerned the creation of a new terrace near the Grotto that was to be planted with American honey locusts (*Gleditsia triacanthos*).

When William died, on 24 November 1848, ownership of Melbourne Hall passed to his brother Frederic and thereafter to their sister Emily (1787– 1869) who at that time was married to Lord Palmerston. Emily owned Melbourne for sixteen years and, although she never lived there, she held it in high regard. After visiting the estate in August 1853, she wrote that 'really this place is quite lovely and the more I see of it, the more I admire it'. However, since she also had use of the country estates at Panshanger and Brocket Hall in Hertfordshire, and her husband Lord Palmerston's house at Broadlands in Hampshire, Emily decided to lease out the Hall. She wrote to her agent instructing him to show the estate to 'any party likely to take it, and who does not want to see it from mere curiosity', and by April 1854 one Mr Briscoe had been approved as a suitable tenant.

Briscoe appears to have appreciated the gardens every bit as much as the house, and he wrote on a number of occasions to make requests for their enhancement. Several notes have survived in which Emily gave her written approval of his suggestions, including the construction of a new Vinery and the removal of an elm tree to improve the view. In a letter dated 27 July 1855, Emily writes that 'Mr Briscoe should do what he likes about the Peacocks. I can have no wish that he should keep them if he finds them troublesome'.

By the end of September that same year, she was approving more extensive alterations. 'I told Mr Briscoe that he might cut down some of the Poplars in the Island and Trees in the Slip under the Terrace by the Water . . . I think Mr Briscoe has evidently very good taste.'

Mr Briscoe left Melbourne Hall in the winter of 1857–58 and a new tenant arrived in the spring of 1858. Colonel Gooch was a distinguished veteran of the Battle of Waterloo and the Melbourne land agent, Frederick Fox, was favourably impressed by him. He was, Fox wrote, 'likely to be a good tenant and to keep up the Gardens just as they are. I should not like them to be spoilt or neglected.'

However, when Colonel Gooch asked permission to remove twenty-four ducks, perhaps citing the mess they left on the lawns, Fox did express some concern: 'I am surprised that finding [the ducks] there, he should not have been glad to keep them. If he is too careful of manure, his Garden will fail [for] the want of it but that is his own affair, and he is bound to keep up the Garden in a proper state.' Other requests, however, were met with a more positive reaction. In September 1858, Fox wrote to say 'I have no objection to the Weeping Ashes on the Parterre being cut down as Col. Gooch wishes it, for in truth I have always thought that they interfered with the regular plan of the garden.'

Colonel Gooch organized at least one fete in the Melbourne Hall gardens, which raised £53 for repairs to the Melbourne parish church, and repeatedly invited Emily to visit her estate.

Right Robert Bakewell's elegant balustrading at the end of the upper terrace.

Opposite top The Pool was extensively remodelled by the first Lord Melbourne, working with landscape gardener William Pontey, who created the two islands in 1845.

Opposite bottom It was Pontey who designed a curved breast wall for the weir and set stones into its surface in a pattern designed to make the falling water tinkle melodically.

Right Shrouded in heavy mist, the wooded islands on the Pool have a mysterious, ethereal atmosphere.

Opposite The pair of iron baskets set into the main lawn were an ornamental addition made by Lord Melbourne, and today are bedded out according to season.

These carefully laid plans were invariably thwarted by the demands of her husband's political career, although the seventy-five-year-old Emily and her seventy-seven-year-old husband did pay a fleeting visit to Melbourne in 1862.

This seems to have been the last time that Emily came to the Hall in person, but she continued to take an interest in the estate. In 1866 there was a problem with weed on the Pool and Emily wrote to Fox with some observations on the subject, including the fact that 'Lord Stanhope says he has known this horrid weed to be destroy'd by turning out several Swans on the water.' A few days later, she wrote again to say, 'I hope you have taken care in lowering the Water of the Pool not to hurt the health of those who surround it.'

Colonel Gooch died in January 1867, and his life and distinguished military career are commemorated by several large stained-glass windows in the chancel of the parish church that were installed by his wife, who stayed on at the Hall and continued to take an interest in the gardens. She requested permission to build a Conservatory, and Emily was keen to keep her valued tenant happy:

> *19 January 1868 . . . I have no objection to the Conservatory but it should not join on the Evidence Room [another name for the Muniment Room, or former dovecot] for fear of fire. In one place you said it would join on to the Dining Room. With all the agreements you propose it cannot be objectionable and it would seem not handsome to refuse her the pleasure of building this Conservatory if she wishes it.*

In 1869 Mrs Gooch invited Lady Palmerston to visit her at Melbourne Hall, but Emily regretfully declined. 'I have so much to do . . . that I am afraid I shall not be able to accept Mrs Gooch's kind invitation . . . If I felt up to such a Journey it would have given me great pleasure to see Melbourne again with all its improvements.' Two weeks later, on 11 September 1869, Emily passed away.

When Emily died the hereditary line passed to the offspring of her first husband, Earl Cowper, but no one from the family lived in the Hall until 1905, when their great-granddaughter Lady Amabel Cowper (1846–1906) inherited. Although she was nearly 60 at the time, Lady Amabel immediately moved in with her husband Lord Walter Kerr, and Melbourne Hall has been a main Kerr family home ever since.

Amabel only survived for a year after moving to Melbourne, but Lord Walter (1839–1927) continued to live in the house until his death, and built the Roman Catholic church in the town in memory of his devout wife. He also made a number of changes to the garden planting between 1905 and the start of the war in 1914, and put in a *claire-voie* at one end of the main upper terrace beside the house. This involved creating a lower section of wall topped by railings to give views out over the Pool and across to a temple folly that stood on rising land on the far side.

He was succeeded by their son Captain Andrew Kerr (1877–1929) and his wife Marie, although like his mother before him, Andrew did not have long to enjoy his inheritance. He died two years later, but his wife went on to live in the Hall for over half a century. Their son Peter Kerr, Twelfth Marquess of Lothian (1922–2004) was brought up at Melbourne Hall and lived there with his wife Antonella for a number of years before moving to a family estate in Scotland. Their son, Ralph (b. 1957), is the current incumbent and lives at Melbourne Hall with his wife Marie-Claire.

Later Visitors

Below The unusually well-preserved historic layout which delights modern day visitors, has always been appreciated by paying guests.

Opposite top The style of dress, and details of planting, may have changed since these engravings were made in the 1870s, but the essence of the garden is remarkably unchanged.

Opposite bottom The winged statue of Mercury on the lower lawn is instantly recognizable, but close inspection of the lawns nearer to the house show evidence of an ornamental parterre planting scheme.

In 1874, the renowned travel-company entrepreneur Thomas Cook, who had been born into a poor Melbourne family, applied to take on the lease of the Hall. It was speculated in the local press that he, 'with noble disregard of broken bottles, sandwich papers, and empty fuzee boxes', might make the gardens a rival to Alton Towers. Cook denied this in a public letter, yet in the same letter set out his dream that Melbourne should become a tourist destination warranting a grand hotel, and that the spring water in the little grotto might 'be turned to useful purpose for invalids or the dyspeptics'. He also said that he would like to introduce exotic plants and birds to the gardens. These ideas tended to substantiate the very fears that his letter set out to dispel. His application was met with genteel distaste and his aspiration to end his days in the largest house of the parish, having begun in one of the tiniest, was roundly thwarted.

Nevertheless, by 1953 the house and gardens were regularly opening to paying visitors. At this time Melbourne Hall was home to Ralph's grandmother, Mrs Andrew Kerr. She had moved into the hall in 1927 and, although her husband died just two years later, she continued to live there until her death in 1980. Mrs Andrew enjoyed welcoming the visitors who came every day from April until the end of September and would herself often show them around. Family legend has it that on one occasion, she had just been out into the garden to pick some salad for lunch when she was urgently called away to speak to someone. For want of anywhere better to hide the lettuce she had been holding from the groups of visitors wandering around, she tucked it into a pretty enamel-lidded box that which then, as now, sat on a bureau in the drawing room. There it remained, forgotten, until its gently decaying remains were inadvertently revealed by an unsuspecting tour guide showing off the box to a later group of visitors.

Whether the story is true or not, it does fit in with the surprisingly domesticated atmosphere of this decidedly grand property. When Ralph and Marie-Claire's six children were small, visitors would often discover toys in the corridors, footballs on the lawns and home-made cards slipped cheekily into the racks of mementos for sale.

In recent years, the estate has diversified again to make the estate available to an even wider range of people. The various ancient outbuildings in the courtyard, which once housed the estate workshops, now contain a range of shops, the Sitooterie coffee stand and a craft brewery, as well as the tearoom just outside the garden gate.

These days the house is only open in the month of August, but the gardens welcome visitors from April to October and, rather than resenting the intrusion, Marie-Claire says she relishes the opportunity to share the fruits of her labours with the widest possible audience. 'When I see people enjoying the gardens, it makes all the hard work feel worthwhile.'

Chapter 9
A New Chapter

Opposite The hand of an accomplished artist is evident in Marie-Claire's elegant floral additions to the outer sections of the gardens, such as this exquisite combination of yellow *Paeonia x lemoinei* 'High Noon' and palest lavender *Iris* 'Melbourne Hall Ghost'.

The most recent chapter of Melbourne Hall's horticultural history began in 1987, when young artist Marie-Claire Black married Ralph, the man she had met when commissioned to paint his brother-in-law's portrait several years earlier.

At that time the gardens were being meticulously maintained, respectful of the historic layout and main features that had been put in place by Thomas Coke at the start of the eighteenth century, but no garden can remain the same from one year to the next, let alone over the course of three centuries. On closer inspection, the passage of time was all too evident in a general and gentle expansion – of lawns across gravel paths, of overhanging branches in the tree-lined avenues and, quite gloriously, in the undulating and enormous walls of yew that framed the formal heart of the garden.

Less appealing were the over-large golden yews and western red cedars (*Thuja plicata*) that ran down either side of the central path from the house, interrupting the view out over the Great Basin and on to the rising parkland beyond. There was also a messy mass of yew, holly and rhododendron (*Rhododendron ponticum*) that had self-seeded into the wilder areas of the main garden.

Like any young bride, Marie-Claire was keen to make her mark on her new family home, harnessing an eye for colour and proportion honed over her many years of artistic training, and a passion for gardens fostered through a childhood spent in her parents' glorious gardens in Cornwall and Scotland. Although still in her early twenties, she set to work with a clear vision and great enthusiasm.

In those first days she was helped enormously by Ken Hicklin, who was then head gardener but had started work in the gardens as a teenager in the 1940s. There was an enormous amount for Marie-Claire to take on board but, undaunted, she immediately started work. Even though her first child arrived shortly afterwards, to be followed in due course by another five, she continued to expand her curatorial interest in the gardens, driven by the creative desire to make a fresh mark of her own.

'I always wanted the gardens to be as botanically stimulating as they were horticulturally interesting,' she says. In part, this took the form of tree planting in various locations around the garden. In consultation with Robert Vernon, of the renowned Bluebell Nursery and Arboretum, she selected some exceptional, choice trees, including a number of interesting oaks and limes that have now grown into magnificent specimens. After some deliberation she planted a Dawyck beech (*Fagus sylvatica* 'Dawyck'), which had been a gift from her mother, in a spot set off to one side of the

Right Marie-Claire is also an enthusiastic and knowledgeable dendrophile, and has added some fine specimens to the gardens, considering the ornamental impact of foliage such as these autumnal lime leaves, as well as the height and form of each tree.

Opposite The Dawyck beech (*Fagus sylvatica* 'Dawyck') was a gift from Marie-Claire's mother and has been given a prominent position behind the yew hedges that frame the Birdcage, where its compact, columnar form can be fully appreciated.

Birdcage where, in time, she imagined it would rise up to form an eye-catching feature.

'Inevitably I made a few mistakes when choosing what to plant where in those early days, and in due course some things I planted had to go, but thankfully not my mother's beautiful beech. She passed away many years ago, and I now doubly cherish it both as a beautiful tree and as a lovely reminder of her.'

Over the years, Marie-Claire has planted a great number of captivating trees and shrubs around the garden but, as a life-long dendrophile, she also began to develop an arboretum in an area to the east of the main connecting route known as the Crow Walk. Here she could 'garden' with trees in a style that was sympathetic to the spirit of Thomas's original garden plan. However, still the artist within her longed for a space where she could play with a much broader spectrum of colour.

Very quickly, Marie-Claire identified an overgrown area to the south of the Yew Tunnel where a series of ornamental plantings might be sensitively created. Full of self-seeded laurel, rhododendron (*Rhododendron ponticum*) and holly, and bisected by streams, it was very far from a blank canvas, and had been the setting for wonderfully wild childhood games when Ralph was a little boy. 'This was a place he visited often as a child, when his grandmother lived here, and he always loved it but, fortunately for me, he has been magnificently supportive and prepared to embrace change,' says Marie-Claire. She venerates the sense of tradition at Melbourne Hall but sees no reason why that should limit the scope for innovation.

Tractors were sent in to clear the site while Marie-Claire continued to refine her vision of the new ornamental garden that would soon fill this space. For the first time in its long history, Melbourne Hall was about to accommodate a herbaceous border in a form that the original artist-gardener Gertrude Jekyll would have recognized and approved. 'I began with the Bog Garden, which I decided to plant in soft but fresh shades of yellow and blue. This was the first time I had set out to design an entire herbaceous border, which was rather daunting, but I approached it like the painting of a picture, considering the combination of flower colour, leaf shape and overall structure of each plant to create a living tapestry.

My art teacher used to get so cross if you started work on a portrait by painting one eye with a small brush. He said you had to start with a huge brush and set down a sense of the whole thing. Only then could you go back and work at the details. I think exactly the same rule applies when you plant up a garden.'

To the Bog Garden beds were soon added the Millstream Borders, which frame the old stream in a haze of soft lemon and pale lilac, and a long ribbon bed in shades of pink that is named for the foxglove tree (*Paulownia tomentosa*) that sits at one end. Within the predominantly green gardens at Melbourne, these

Left The Crow Walk is one of the longest vistas in the whole garden, and for hundreds of years visitors have strolled its length in the dappled shade of the surrounding trees.

Left The view along the Crow Walk to the Fountain Walk, the Four Seasons Urn and the Nine Pins is essentially unchanged since Thomas Coke's day, although the flanking yew hedges have broadened and bulged considerably over time.

colourful beds glow like a basket of rare jewels spread out to tempt those who stroll in the outer reaches of the gardens, in much the same way that Thomas Coke set out his fountains, urns and avenues to attract the attention of garden visitors three centuries ago.

Every great garden is ephemeral. Day by day, it is shaped by someone who cares passionately about it and is willing to devote themselves to realizing in physical form their emotional and creative response to the possibilities of the place. Thomas Coke did this when he first laid out the Melbourne Hall gardens at the start of the eighteenth century, and Marie-Claire does the same thing today. 'A garden is a moment in time,' she says. 'It has to constantly evolve if you are to keep its original spirit alive.'

Opposite The Bog Garden is fed by a spring which rises up within the grotto, and its crystal-clear waters frame banks covered in the lovely golden-flowered candelabra primula (*Primula prolifera*).

Above The Millstream Borders are a romantic set piece that calls to mind Claude Monet's gardens at Giverny. Great stands of creamy *Hydrangea arborescens* 'Annabelle' and lavender-flowered hostas contribute to the picture.

Right Looking along the Millstream Borders towards the bridge, and the Paulownia Border beyond, the view is lush, romantic and perfectly judged.

The Winter Garden

Below *Hamamelis × intermedia* 'Jelena' is a vigorous witch hazel which produces sweetly scented burnt-orange flowers on its winter-bare twigs.

Opposite top Marie-Claire has created a charming Winter Garden, enclosed by the Muniment Room and surrounding hedges, where the scent of a selection of winter-flowering shrubs can be truly appreciated.

Opposite bottom left *Daphne bholua* 'Jacqueline Postill' has also been planted in this dedicated space, and its perfume is intoxicating on a cold, crisp day, although it is a relatively slow-growing cultivar.

Opposite bottom right Not every plant in the Winter Garden is fragrant. Marie-Claire has also amassed a collection of colourful hellebores to brighten these beds in the cold, dark days at the start of each year.

Paying visitors to the garden enter via a small gate thickly coated in green paint. It feels a little like walking into Frances Hodgson Burnett's secret garden, except that what greets you on the other side is not a romantically overgrown jungle but a quiet green space with a surprisingly intimate feel.

To one side is the curious hexagonal building called the Muniment Room, which has stood on this spot since at least 1629, when it was clearly highlighted in a garden plan drawn up for the first Sir John Coke. Four hundred years ago, it was called the 'Dove Cote' and would have provided eggs and squab pigeons that were destined to end up being cooked in the Hall kitchens. At the start of the eighteenth century, Thomas Coke turned the building into a Muniment Room, where he could store all his important papers, and it has remained essentially unchanged to the present day. The thick stone walls are made of local stone giving the little building, with its unusual and very lovely bell-shaped roof, a reassuring solidity. Until very recently root vegetables were stored here through the winter, in a low chamber that is reached down a shallow external flight of steps that are still clearly visible.

The real change in this area is the Winter Garden that Marie-Claire began to develop twenty years ago. Edged by stones wrapped in a velvety coat of moss and backed by the bulging sides of a yew hedge, this garden has a real picture-book charm and sense of great intimacy.

There is a selection of well-chosen winter-interest shrubs, many of them fragrant, including the lovely burnt orange witch hazel (*Hamamelis* x *intermedia* 'Jelena'), the winter honeysuckle (*Lonicera* x *purpusii* 'Winter Beauty'), and the extremely lovely *Daphne bholua* 'Jacqueline Postill'. The visually insignificant white flowers of the sweet box (*Sarcococca confusa*), add to the cloud of perfume that fills the air on still, cold days.

The Siberian dogwood, *Cornus alba* 'Sibirica', is carefully cut down close to the ground every spring in order to stimulate the production of fresh new stems that, by the following winter, will positively glow with bold stripes of vivid red. Two large specimens of *Hydrangea paniculata* have also been skilfully pruned, this time to maximize the elegance of their silhouette, which is smothered in panicles of flowers all summer. As the rest of the garden settles into winter dormancy, these blooms fade to tawny skeletons of their former selves, which retain a rich warmth all through the winter, complementing the mellow stone of the Muniment Room and contrasting with the solid-green backdrop of the carefully clipped yew hedge.

At their feet, clumps of snowdrops are wound through a riot of hellebores, including *Helleborus* x *ericsmithii* HGC Monte Christo, and cyclamens in delicious bonbon colours brighten the dark earth. Compared with the scale of the rest of the gardens, this is a decidedly modest set piece, but it works as a perfect *amuse-bouche* for visitors preparing to walk down the Library Walk towards the glorious formal heart of the Melbourne Hall estate.

The bell-shaped roof of the Muniment Room, a decorative flourish which Thomas Coke added to a much older structure, is a distinctive feature of the gardens.

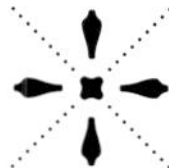

Chapter 10
Painterly Plantings

Opposite The herbaceous borders to the south of the main lawns gave Marie-Claire a place where she could exercise her artistic eye for colour.

'Tending and extending this garden has been like painting a picture that changes every day – in fact it sometimes feels like someone else secretly adds bits to it in the middle of the night,' says Marie-Claire.

When Marie-Claire moved to Melbourne Hall she found herself living in a garden that was unquestionably beautiful, but botanically rather lacking in interest and coloured predominantly in different shades of green. As an artist, she craved a more varied palette and a space away from the perfectly staged, formal heart of the garden where she could create something new. She found the perfect location beyond the south side of the Yew Tunnel, where the ancient millstream flowed, although at that time sections of it were almost completely hidden from sight by a mass of self-sown holly, sycamore and rhododendron (*Rhododendron ponticum*).

As soon as the site was cleared, she set to work on the rich damp soil, first creating a Bog Garden in the dappled shade of some statuesquely beautiful overhanging trees. She was just twenty-five years old and, although she had been fortunate enough to grow up surrounded by wonderful plants, she had no first-hand experience of combining them to create a whole new garden. 'In the early days I was hugely helped and guided by Robert Vernon and, particularly on the herbaceous side, by his wonderful wife Suzette. I still managed to make so many mistakes to start off with, but I was driven by passion. Initially I was drawn to all the beautiful spring-interest flowers, from rhododendrons to candelabra primulas. Some, like my first Rhododendron macabeanum, I put in the wrong place, where it completely failed to thrive until I realized and moved it. With the candelabra primulas, I let my collector's enthusiasm get the better of me and initially put far too many different colours together. As I have grown older and more experienced, I have realized that simplicity is usually the key to a successful scheme.'

With her innate understanding of colour honed by years of artistic training and professional painting, Marie-Claire decided upon a spring-fresh combination of yellow and blue in the Bog Garden. Elegant Cockburnia primroses and other candelabra forms were visually enhanced by vivid 'Blue Heron' corydalis, while lime-green hostas perfectly set off the blue *Meconopsis* poppies that she had first come to love as a child in Scotland. Into the mix she added a handkerchief tree (*Davidia involucrata*) and a paperbark maple (*Acer griseum*), visualizing how the cinnamon tones of the acer would enhance the overall picture in the years to come.

Around the adjacent grotto, she set a dainty little white rose scrambling over the roof and let Turk's cap lilies self-

Above It is easy to discern the hand of an artist in many of the border schemes, which swirl broad strokes of soft colour together to produce an impossibly romantic picture.

Right Although Marie-Claire is proficient at gardening on the grand scale, as an artist she is also adept at selecting individual plants of great delicacy and charm, such as this pretty pink *Diascia personata* 'Hopleys'.

Opposite A young wedding cake tree (*Cornus controversa* 'Variegata'), with its distinctive tiered shape, forms an interesting visual contrast with the spires of pineapple lily (*Eucomis comosa*) and and a sprawling, soft pink diascia.

Left Marie-Claire is equally confident working with a palette of different greens, as in this streamside combination of variegated hostas and *Alchemilla mollis*, with pale astilbes in the foreground and a golden acer standing out against the backdrop of clipped yew hedging.

Above The Bog Garden is the most informal and naturalistic of Marie-Claire's waterside creations, where acers (*A. palmatum* and the paperbark maple *A. griseum*) arch their branches over a delicate combination of flag iris and yellow candelabra primulas.

Opposite top Backlit by spring sunshine, fresh young acer foliage glows richly in this cool green setting, where lavender camassia spires provide the only other touch of contrasting colour.

Opposite bottom The scented yellow azalea (*Rhododendron luteum*) can be invasive, but in this well managed garden it is a lovely addition that complements the low-growing golden flowers of the candelabra primula (*Primula prolifera*).

seed at the skirt of a cushiony mound of the round-leaved *Rhododendron williamsianum*.

Once she started, Marie-Claire found that she couldn't stop, and next turned her attention to a neighbouring area where the light levels were higher and the ground a little drier. Here she created the Paulownia Border and Long Border in an innovative combination of pale pink and dark red, to which the eponymous *Paulownia*, or foxglove tree, adds its soft lavender-pink flowers in April, although the display starts much earlier in the year. First there are assembled masses of tulips, in which the cultivar selection is continually refined and revised, then more of Marie-Claire's beloved primulas. 'For a time, we had them in too many different colours,' says Marie-Claire. 'Now we focus on *Primula pulverulenta* and other pink forms, which have been chosen to complement the general scheme of dark reds and pale pinks.' The herbaceous content builds as the season progresses and includes a wave of 'flowering' dogwood (the showy elements are technically bracts). Later in the year there is a rich display of autumn colour from a number of unusual horse chestnuts and katsuras (*Cercidiphyllums*), among a great deal more besides. Each species is given its moment to shine, and the picture is continually reassessed.

Separated from this richly coloured confection by a broad path of velvety emerald grass, are the Mill Borders, where Marie-Claire has created a hugely romantic picture in sherbet-

Right Working with a broad brush to produce a dramatic effect, Marie-Claire grows *Verbena bonariensis* in front of a stand of *Hydrangea paniculata* 'Limelight' where its vivid purple colour and airy form produce a striking contrast with the dense pinkish panicles behind.

soft shades of lemon, lilac and lime. Here, the decorative effect is further enhanced by the water of the stream itself, which mirrors the exuberantly planted beds tumbling towards it on both sides.

In general, water is a huge element in these gardens – the gentle sound of the fountains, the dragonflies and damselflies that dart everywhere and the newts, frogs, mussels and little fish that live in the water itself. Now, in spirit at least, the Mill Borders recall that other artist's water garden, at Giverny, where Monet planted and painted his waterlilies. At Melbourne Hall, the millstream runs too fast for waterlilies, but the masses of 'Annabelle' hydrangeas, lush clumps of hosta and trailing stems of rambling roses create a reflective picture that is every bit as magical. There are also swathes of an unnamed but very beautiful palest-lavender iris that has become something of a Melbourne Hall signature plant, in much the same way that the clever use of herbaceous colour has become a signature of the gardens as a whole.

Marie-Claire is always delighted to see visitors photographing and debating the plant combinations in these colourful borders, but this is not the only area where she has focussed her creative talents. Beyond the public gaze she has also created a private space intended solely for her family to use that, unsurprisingly, has been given every bit as much creative consideration as the rest of the garden. Here, behind a metal gate set into an arched gateway, the palette is soft shades of bronze

Opposite The fine scented rhododendron 'Loderi King George', which grows in the Long Border, is a particular favourite of Marie-Claire, who has painted it in oils as well as planting it in her garden.

Below The soft pink forms of *Primula pulverulenta* are another of her favourites, grown in a romantic profusion alongside pink foxgloves and the pale spires of *Camassia leichtlinii* 'Semiplena'.

Left The clear fresh colour of the tulip 'Pink Diamond' pairs beautifully with the rich dark tones of the 'Queen of Night' tulip in this charming spring combination.

Above Demonstrating a real understanding of her palette of plants, Marie-Claire framed one millstream with a swathe of the notoriously floppy hydrangea 'Annabelle', where it can drape romantically at the water's edge.

Right The pale pompoms of the 'Annabelle' hydrangeas contrast with the boldly feathered foliage of the royal fern (*Osmunda regalis*) and the deeply cut leaves of a large specimen tree peony.

Opposite These blonde red-crested pochards make an ornamental addition to the crystal-clear waters of the Millstream.

Right In early summer, a carpet of pretty pink candelabra primulas, the scented pink 'Loderi King George' rhododendron and pale camassias are perfectly set off by the distinctive spreading branches of a fine specimen *Viburnum plicatum* covered in white umbels.

Above Looking from the bridge towards the Old Mill, soft mauve bearded iris and yellow tree peony, *Paeonia* 'High Noon' contribute to the lemon and lavender colour theme in this tranquil area.

and lemon that complement the warm tones of the brick walls enclosing this intimate space. Foxtail lilies (*Eremurus*) and the climbing rose 'The Pilgrim', towering giant scabeous (*Cephalaria gigantea*) and a carefully chosen selection of peonies are anchored by sculptural balls of variegated pittosporum and softened with an airy scattering of bronze fennel. The practicalities of life are also catered for. There is a generously proportioned garden table and enough chairs to comfortably seat the entire Kerr clan. There is also a barbecue, set out in a paved corner next to the house that once contained Lord Melbourne's dressing room (look carefully at the walls on this corner of the Hall and you will see the remains of a rendered surface, although the walls that once enclosed it were long ago demolished).

This private garden is known as the Peacock Garden, and it serves as a perfect metaphor for the gardens in general and the estate as a whole. The history of the site has been acknowledged, it is respected, but it has also been enhanced and adapted to the needs of the family who currently call this historic property their home.

Left Water has always been at the heart of the gardens of Melbourne Hall, as a practical resource in the earliest days, but now celebrated as a key ornamental element of the overall picture.

Below Gently shaded by the spreading branches of a cut-leaf beech (*Fagus sylvatica* var. *heterophylla* (Atropurpurea Group) 'Ansorgei'), a thoughtfully sited bench gives visitors an excuse to pause and take in the tranquil scene.

Right The 'Annabelle' hydrangeas maintain their good looks well into autumn, even as their foliage begins to change colour, complementing the golden and russet shades of fading hostas and a lavender fluff of dainty asters.

Above The family's private garden, known as the Peacock Garden, is separated from the public spaces by a gateway wreathed in climbing roses and framed by soft yellow foxtail lilies (*eremurus*), giant scabious (*Cephalaria gigantea*) and peonies.

Right A beautifully trained climbing rose, 'The Pilgrim', covers the brick walls of the private garden with a succession of fragrant soft yellow blooms for many months through the summer.

Opposite A second gateway into the Peacock Garden is framed with more climbing roses and a mass of white Japanese anemones.

Right On the public side of the Peacock Garden walls, the robustly healthy 'Iceberg' rose is paired with a large bed of lavender, in a colour combination that recalls Marie-Claire's Scottish heritage.

Gertrude Jekyll on Artistic Border Design

Opposite Like Marie-Claire, Gertrude Jekyll loved to capture her horticultural creations in pencil and paint, preserving her juxtapositions of spires – here including hollyhocks and spiky yucca flowers – corner markers including bergenias and lavender, and a celebration of colour.

Below The present-day planting scheme in the Peacock Garden, with its spires of foxtail lilies, mounds of roses, and clipped topiary balls, could easily have been assembled by Jekyll.

Over one hundred years ago the original great artist gardener, Gertrude Jekyll, wrote an account of her own approach to border design that could equally well apply to the beautifully colour-themed planting combinations created at Melbourne Hall by Marie-Claire over the last three decades.

> *I am strongly of the opinion that the possession of a quantity of plants, however good the plants may be themselves and however ample their number, does not make a garden; it only makes a collection. Having got the plants, the great thing is to use them with careful selection and definite intention. Merely having them, or having them planted unassorted in garden spaces, is only like having a box of paints from the best colourman, or, to go one step further, it is like having portions of these paints set out upon a palette. This does not constitute a picture; and it seems to me that the duty we owe to our gardens and to our own bettering in our gardens is so to use the plants that they shall form beautiful pictures; and that, while delighting our eyes they should be always training those eyes to a more exalted criticism; to a state of mind and artistic conscience that will not tolerate bad or careless combination or any sort of misuse of plants, but in which it becomes a point of honour to be always striving for the best.*
>
> — Gertrude Jekyll, *Colour in the Flower Garden*, 1908

Chapter 11
Gardening with Trees

Opposite The damp-loving swamp cypress (*Taxodium distichum*) grows happily on the banks of the quadrilobular pond, where it pokes curious knobbly 'knees' (characteristic woody root protuberances) well out into the water.

Thomas Coke bought trees in bulk. His orders to the Brompton Park Nursery of London & Wise would make a shopaholic blush but, reading through these extensive lists, he does not seem to have been a collector of individual specimens of interest. Instead, it appears that his primary concern was with the overall effect that these trees would create.

In the centuries that followed, some of his purchases died while others seeded themselves around. Successive occupants of Melbourne Hall made their own additions and there were also many rogue invaders, introduced in one way or another by visiting wildlife.

All in all, by the time Marie-Claire took over the care of the garden, some trees were nearing the end of their lives, others had grown in a way that spoiled the overall picture, and several significant parts of the garden had become jumbled thickets without any clear botanical merit. Having inherited a love of trees from her Scottish father, Marie-Claire was keen to thoroughly curate what already existed and then to add only the very best specimens in exactly the right places. Her underlying principle was to make use of native trees around the outer limits, and to introduce more refined, cultivated selections within the heart of the garden.

She started slowly, taking stock overall, seeking expert advice in certain areas, and beginning the laborious process of obtaining permits to remove some of the most troublesome specimens. Warned that she might be sent to prison if she removed a particularly intrusive sycamore tree before a long-delayed planning permission had finally been granted, it became part of Kerr family lore when Marie-Claire announced that she would rather be incarcerated than spend another year looking at it.

The great age of the garden throws up constant challenges, even in areas where everyone is quite happy with the existing picture. This is always the challenge when maintaining a historic garden. Plants grow, they mature, and in due course they will die and need to be replaced. Several years ago, a number of large swamp cypresses had to be removed from around the Great Basin because they had reached the end of their life. Keen to recreate the planting, Marie-Claire struggled to source replacement trees of a suitable size, and in the end discovered that the nearest available stock of the same fine form was in Antwerp. Undeterred, she dispatched her estate manager to Belgium to collect them. 'Such landmark trees are too important for me to compromise and settle for second-rate alternatives,' she says.

Some trees, including a number of large copper beeches thought to have been planted in the early 1900s, and a group

of weeping pears that blocked a view of the celebrated van Nost statue of Andromeda, were inappropriate additions to this historic setting. But Marie-Claire does not subscribe to the school of obsessive historicism that advocates planting only trees that were available in the early eighteenth century. The weeping pears, for example, were removed, to free up the view of Andromeda, but two elegantly draping specimens of *Tilia tomentosa* 'Petiolaris', one of Marie-Claire's favourite trees, were planted to frame the Great Basin even though this species was probably not cultivated in England until the mid-nineteenth century.

In other areas, previous indiscriminate tree planting and uncontrolled seeding had obscured the potential of the site, most notably on the rising parkland at the end of the garden, which now sets up such an important vista behind the Birdcage. 'Before we started work on this area, there was only the most eccentric collection of lime trees and scrub in the parkland, none of which were planted in alignment with the garden,' says Marie-Claire. These were primarily *Tilia x europaea* 'Pallida', some of which were dying and others of which were visually diminished by choking weed trees and shrubs when Marie-Claire decided it was time to undertake a serious renovation project. After bat surveys and various other time-consuming conservation processes had been followed, she was finally ready to start planting a formal lime avenue at a serendipitous moment. Her brother-in-law, the Duke of Buccleuch, had been cloning the lime cultivar,

Opposite In the autumn, fallen foliage from the various bankside swamp cypresses (*Taxodium distichum*) and neighbouring oak trees form a floating tapestry of russet tones on the surface of the water.

Above The gracefully arching weeping silver lime (*Tilia tomentosa* 'Petiolaris') grows on the banks of the Great Basin, where it colours attractively in the autumn before losing its foliage for winter.

Left The avenues of pollarded limes have a striking simplicity in winter, when the tracery of their bare branches is silhouetted against the sky.

Above When clothed in foliage, the pollarded limes, with their ground level suckering branches clipped into a neat hedge, form a strongly defined avenue that focuses attention on the magnificent Four Seasons Urn.

Opposite An aerial photograph of the same avenue helps to set the formality of the garden in its wider landscape setting.

Tilia x europaea 'Hatfield Tall' for Boughton House, his own estate in Northamptonshire, and generously gifted Melbourne Hall enough young trees to enable Marie-Claire to realize her vision of a double avenue of limes running away to the horizon.

Marie-Claire has a true collector's zeal for interesting and unusual trees, which she continues to plant around the gardens. The success of this venture owes much to her artistic eye and an almost uncanny ability to visualize the impact a mature tree will have, even as she is positioning a young sapling. 'The first thing is to see the whole picture. Then, within that, work out where you need to concentrate the details, where you need to add colour or strong shapes,' she explains.

Dendrophiles are always delighted by the rare specimens to be found in all quarters of the garden, such as the Daimyo oak (*Quercus dentata* 'Carl Ferris Miller'), with its notably large and felted leaves, and the northern pin oak (*Quercus ellipsoidalis*), which colours a brilliant red in autumn. Some of these are worked into the borders, while others rise out of a series of simple green enclosures framed by yew hedges that fringe the outer avenues around the formal heart of the garden. There are also individual trees of personal significance that have been given prominent positions, including a *Robinia x margaretta* 'Casque Rouge' that was given to Ralph by the estate to mark his fortieth birthday.

But Marie-Claire also dreamed of creating a carefully curated arboretum in an overgrown area to the east of the Fountain Walk.

First the site had to be cleared of laurel and carpets of nettles, then the ground was drained to improve growing conditions and increase the potential range of trees from which she could choose. At that time, the north end of the arboretum was largely obscured by an overgrown extension to the Yew Tunnel and, as her vision for this area became clearer, she decided to reduce the overall length of the tunnel to return it to the dimensions set out by Thomas Coke in his original master plan.

Keen to avoid unseen pitfalls she contacted Robert Vernon, the specialist behind the renowned Bluebell Arboretum and Nursery. 'It was so exciting going around making plans with Robert. I was just twenty-five when we very first started – I began work on this part of the garden even before I thought about what to do with the house.'

The trees were loosely grouped by species, always with Marie-Claire's artistic eye visualizing how the light would fall and filter once the leaf canopy neared maturity. There is a stunning specimen red oak (*Quercus rubra* 'Aurea'), a gift from Robert Vernon, that she has planted near the quadrilobular pool to the east of the Fountain Walk that is a great example of this picture-building. It is positioned to be perfectly aligned behind the sparkling fountain spout when you walk towards it from the commemorative Melbourne Urn. 'Of course, this is the challenge with gardening on any scale – visualizing the impact of a planting scheme in its future maturity. But with herbaceous

Opposite Marie-Claire applies her artistic eye to the selection and positioning of trees with every bit as much care as her herbaceous plantings. This swamp cypress (*Taxodium distichum*) is well suited to its damp waterside site, and the fiery colour of its autumnal foliage is a striking counterpoint to the 'smalt blue' and gilded Birdcage.

Above left Other choice trees, such as this rare Daimyo oak (*Quercus dentata* 'Carl Ferris Miller'), are displayed within enclosures of yew hedging.

Above right The leaves of *Quercus dentata* 'Carl Ferris Miller' are unusually large, with a distinctively thick, felted texture, and turn to rich shades of buttery yellow in autumn.

Right The ring of pollarded lime trees known as the Nine Pins, are underplanted with a dainty sprinkle of 'White Triumphator' tulips rising up out of long meadow grass.

Above In her Arboretum, Marie-Claire is developing a tapestry lawn that includes deep purple 'Queen of Night' and 'Recreado' tulips and pale lavender camassias.

Right *Quercus rubra* 'Evenley Gold', a particularly handsome form of red oak, with golden leaves, has soft golden-green leaves in summer which turn pink and red in autumn.

Opposite top left *Liriodendron × sinoamericanum* 'Chapel Hill', a choice hybrid between the American and Chinese tulip trees, has a neat habit and from a relatively early age bears striking copper-green flowers in midsummer.

Opposite top right *Cornus controversa* 'Variegata' is a beautiful small tree that begins to develop its distinctive tiered branches after a couple of years, and Marie-Claire has planted it both in the Arboretum and the Long Border.

Opposite bottom Marie-Claire is used to gardening on a grand scale, and has arranged her Arboretum in much the same way that other people lay out borders, with certain specimen trees planted in groups, and a stone urn positioned as an eye-catcher.

Right At the tail end of winter, the Arboretum sparkles with a shimmering mass of the tiny common snowdrop (*Galanthus nivalis*).

Above The handkerchief tree (*Davidia involucrata*) is native to south-west China but looks completely at home in the Dell at Melbourne Hall, where its distinctive dangling flower bracts flutter gently on breezy days in May and June.

Right A mature plane tree rises at a rakish angle out of a pungent but pretty carpet of the flowering wild garlic (*Allium ursinum*).

Opposite There is some evidence of historic plans to flood the Dell with an ornamental water feature, but instead it has remained as a quiet wooded area dappled with sunlight.

planting and most shrubs, you can at least move them if you realize you haven't quite got it right first time. It isn't completely impossible to do the same thing with a tree, but it does take considerably more effort.'

Today, the consequence of this obsessive attention to detail is gloriously apparent. There is a fine pair of *Tilia henryana*, three nicely spaced tulip trees (*Liriodendron*) and another loose group of three dogwood. In fact, Marie-Claire often plants her trees in threes and fives, in much the same way that a domestic gardener might plan a border, to maximize their ornamental impact. Each new planting is thought about and discussed for several weeks, then placed very precisely. There is always a picture being made. It makes a refreshing change from so many arboreta, where obsessive tree-collectors cram in as many different specimens as they dare, giving little thought for the space required by each mature individual, let alone its cumulative visual impact.

With the main elements of her arboretum in place, Marie-Claire began embroidering the understorey, sprinkling the ground with white and mauve chequered snake's-head fritillaries and pale blue scillas. These are closely followed by the more cultivated delights of deep purple tulips 'Queen of Night' and 'Recreado' that push up through the lengthening grass alongside pale azure flowered camassia and the lovely double white 'Semiplena' form. *Epimedium* 'Pink Elf' makes an unusual path edging through the arboretum and, later in the year, there are colchicum and autumn cyclamen.

Most recently, Marie-Claire has been choosing trees to enhance the shady area by the southern boundary that is known as the Dell. Everything here has a white leaf, white bark or a silver variegation, including the lovely *Fagus sylvatica* 'Franken', a dwarf beech with white variegated leaves that echo the effect of dappled sunlight filtering through the tree canopy.

'I love my trees,' says Marie-Claire. 'As much as their wonderful silhouettes, I value the colour of their leaves, the texture and tone of the bark, and those flowering trees which can give you an extra seasonal hit of colour and interest. This garden wouldn't be the same without them.'

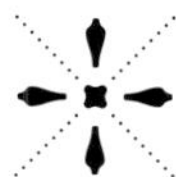

Chapter 12
Future Plans

Opposite Like the water that has flowed through the grounds at Melbourne Hall for centuries, the gardens are both essentially unchanged and endlessly in flux.

No garden can stand still, and nor will it ever be finished. Marie-Claire has achieved a huge amount in the decades that she has overseen the gardens at Melbourne Hall, and she regularly reappraises and enhances the significant ornamental areas that she has already created, but she is also constantly dreaming up new visions to enhance the overall picture.

One of her more recent projects is a completely new blue-and-white planting scheme for the deep border that runs along the upper terrace. Here she has created a formal display of irises, white alliums and 'Kew Gardens' roses trained up iron frames, among a great deal more besides. Structure comes from pittosporum balls and an edge of low box hedges, and the overall display is framed in sections by tall yew buttresses that tie in with the formality of the house front.

Another project involves structure of a more concrete and tangible variety. Having long ago returned the Birdcage to its former glory, framed by a crescent of yews that anchors it into its setting, Marie-Claire is now finally realizing a long-held ambition to physically connect it back to the parkland that rises on the far side of Carr Brook, the fast flowing stream immediately outside the end wall of the garden.

There is a small door at the back of the Birdcage that was bricked over for many decades, blocking any direct access to the parkland. Marie-Claire had this doorway reopened and installed a temporary bridge of railway sleepers across the brook, replacing the previous bridge that was washed away in floods in 1932. The original bridge is now being restored, and at the time of writing is very close to completion. The finishing touch will be a small drawbridge, created to a design by Ralph, which can be raised to symbolically secure this hidden perimeter.

As if that were not enough, the indefatigable Marie-Claire is also currently overseeing the completion of a magnificent walled Rose Garden in a large plot of land framed by two of Thomas Coke's original brick fruit walls. This had lost its purpose after the Second World War, when the scale of productive horticulture was slimmed from its labour-intensive heyday, until Ralph's mother, Lady Lothian, instructed the construction of two end walls to create a secret, sunny garden away from the eyes of the visiting public.

At one time there was talk of putting in a swimming pool, but it was just a simple rectangle of mown grass when Marie-Claire began to dream of roses. The picture she had in her mind was part English-country idyll, and part something closer to the Paradise Gardens of the Alhambra, with a sunken central stone-edged rill containing three fountains in reference to the three fountain pools in the main garden. This has been framed with

Right The gardens that she has nurtured for almost four decades are a constant source of inspiration to Marie-Claire, both as a gardener and as an artist.

Left As a direct descendant of Thomas Coke, Ralph now stacks his beloved musical recordings on shelves erected by his ancestors, and reads in view of a venerable Atlas cedar (*Cedrus atlantica*) that would have been familiar to many of them.

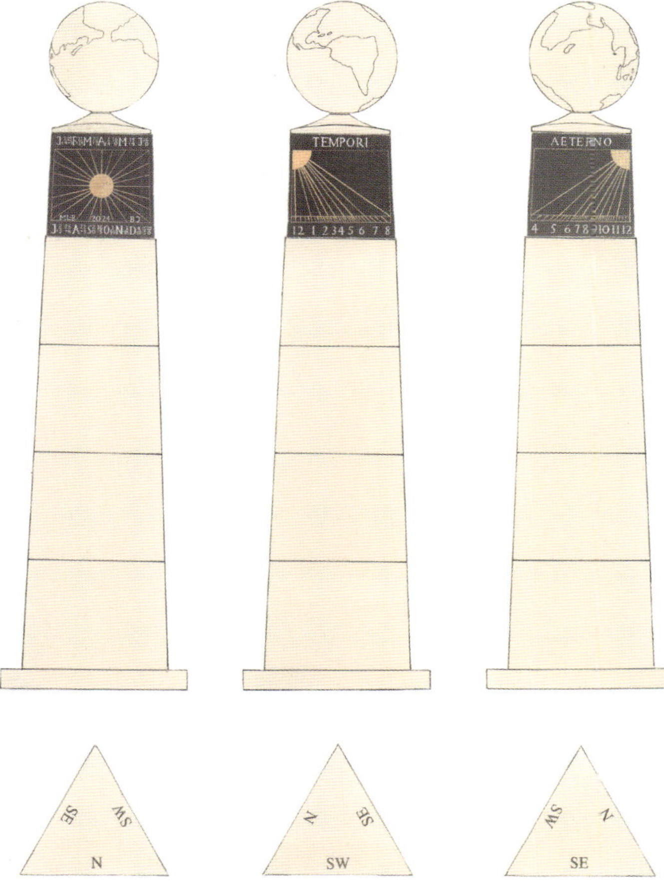

variegated pittosporum and masses of pure white roses, while the outer walls, accessed by two elegant flights of stone steps, are a kaleidoscope of colour.

Here the gardener-artist is currently conjuring another of her picture-perfect planting plans, despite the practical difficulties of creating a unified scheme in a space where one long wall faces due south and the other looks north. These diametrically opposite aspects made it impossible to simply grow matched pairs of roses down each long side of the garden, since some cultivars will simply not perform in lower light levels. Instead, Marie-Claire has worked hard to find varieties suited to each different site that will, in time, cover the walls with a coherent swirl of softly modulating colour.

'You have to be brave and forward moving in a garden like this,' she says. 'It is a bit like raising my six children. You need military precision to keep the show on the road, but you must also remain loose and expansive enough to allow room for elaboration, and have enough love to allow each of your charges to develop their own individual potential.'

Opposite One of the more recent interventions has been the construction, to an original design by Ralph, of a new drawbridge across Carr Brook that leads from a small door at the back of the Birdcage out into the Park.

Above left In a new garden enclosed by Thomas Coke's original fruit walls, Marie-Claire is now bringing her artist's eye to bear on the design of a dedicated Rose Garden with a contemporary rill at its heart, which recalls the enduring importance of water to the Melbourne Hall estate.

Above right Designs for a sundial by Mark Lennox-Boyd, planned to be installed at the end of the new Rose Garden.

Overleaf The sun rises above the gilded dome of the Birdcage, as it has every day for hundreds of years, glinting on the still water of the Great Basin in a scene that would be as familiar to Thomas Coke as it is to those descendants of his family line who call Melbourne Hall their home today.

Index

Captions to illustrations are indicated by page numbers in *italics*. Feature articles are indicated by page numbers in **bold**.

Bibliography

Beard, Geoffrey W., *Georgian Craftsmen and Their Work* (Country Life, 1966)

Blomfield, Reginald and Thomas, Francis Inigo, *The Formal Garden in England* (Macmillan, 1892)

Cecil, David, *The Young Melbourne & Lord M* (Pan Macmillan, 2017)

Eburne, Andrew and Taylor, Richard, *How to Read an English Garden* (Ebury, 2016)

Fiennes, Celia, *Through England on a Side Saddle in the Time of William and Mary: Being the Diary of Celia Fiennes* (Field and Tuer, 1888)

Green, David Brontë, *Gardener to Queen Anne: Henry Wise (1653–1738) and the Formal Garden* (Oxford University Press, 1956)

Gunnis, Rupert, *Dictionary of British Sculptors, 1660–1851* (Odhams Press, 1953)

Hagglund, Elizabeth, 'Cassandra Willougby's Visits to Country Houses' in *The Georgian Group Report & Journal* vol. 11 (2001)

Heath, Philip, 'Melbourne Hall Reconsidered' in *The Georgian Group Report & Journal* (1988).

Hook, Judith, *The Baroque Age in England* (Thames and Hudson, 1976)

Hunt, John Dixon, *Garden and Grove: The Italian Renaissance Garden and the English Imagination 1600–1750* (Princeton University Press, 1986)

Hussey, Christopher Edward Clive, *English Gardens and Landscapes 1700–1750* (Country Life, 1967)

Jacques, David, *Gardens of Court and Country: English Design 1630–1730* (Yale University Press, 2017)

Jekyll, Gertrude, *Colour in the Flower Garden* (Timber Press, 1995)

Kelly, E.R., *Kelly's Directory of Derbyshire, Leicestershire & Rutland, and Nottinghamshire* (London, 1891)

Lister, Raymond, *Decorative Wrought Ironwork in Great Britain* (Bell and Sons, 1957).

Manuscripts of the Earl Cowper KG preserved at Melbourne Hall, *Historical Manuscripts Commission* Vol, 3 (1889)

'Melbourne Hall' in *Country Life* (23 September 1899)

'Melbourne Hall' in *Country Life* (7 and 14 April 1928)

Morris, Christopher (ed.), *The Illustrated Journeys of Celia Fiennes, 1685–*c.*1712* (Macdonald, 1982)

Mowl, Timothy, *Gentlemen & Players: Gardeners of the English Landscape* (Sutton Publishing, 2000)

Schmidt, Leo, Keller, Christian and Feversham, Polly (eds), *Holkham* (Prestel, 2005)

Strong, Roy, *The Renaissance Garden in England* (Thames and Hudson, 1998)

Thacker, Christopher, *The History of Gardens* (Reed, 1979)

Thomas, Graham Stuart, *Gardens of the National Trust* (National Trust, 1979)

Turner, Tom, *English Garden Design: History and Styles Since 1650* (Antique Collectors' Club, 1986)

Uglow, Jenny, *A Little History of British Gardening* (Pimlico, 2005)

Ziegler, Philip, *Melbourne: A Biography of William Lamb, 2nd Viscount Melbourne* (Faber & Faber, 2013)

Picture credits

All images © Andrea Jones except:

8–9: Melbourne Hall
18: Melbourne Hall
33: microman6/Getty Images
37 above: BTEU/RKMLGE/Alamy Stock Photo
37 below: National Gallery of Ireland Collection
50: adoc-photos/Getty Images
52: Harris Brisbane Dick Fund, 1926, The Metropolitan Museum of Art/Public Domain
53 above: Hulton Archive/Getty Images
53 below: Print Collector/Getty Images
54–55: Royal Collection Trust/© His Majesty King Charles III, 2025/Bridgeman Images
56: Rogers Fund, 1952, The Metropolitan Museum of Art/Public Domain
57: Antiqua Print Gallery/Alamy Stock Photo
73 above: Melbourne Hall
79: Heritage Image Partnership Ltd/Alamy Stock Photo
118: The Picture Art Collection/Alamy Stock Photo
129: Pictorial Press Ltd/Alamy
133: © Look and Learn/Bridgeman Images
145 above: Sepia Times/Getty Images
145 below: Sepia Times/Getty Images
188: © Mallett Gallery, London, UK/Bridgeman Images

Thanks

Writing this book involved a huge amount of primary research and I am indebted to Philip Heath, archivist at Melbourne Hall, without whose patient and expert assistance I might have been permanently lost in a pile of antique paperwork.

I am also extremely grateful to architectural and garden historian Dr Sally Jeffery, FSA, who generously gave up her time to read the final manuscript of this book.

Finally, I would like to thank Ralph and Marie-Claire, for giving me the opportunity to write about their extraordinary garden.

Quarto

First published in 2025 by Frances Lincoln,
an imprint of The Quarto Group.
One Triptych Place
London, SE1 9SH, United Kingdom
T (0)20 7700 9000
www.Quarto.com

EEA Representation, WTS Tax d.o.o., Žanova ulica 3, 4000 Kranj, Slovenia.
www.wts-tax.si

A catalogue record for this book is available from the British Library.

ISBN 978-0-7112-8297-1
Ebook ISBN 978-0-7112-8298-8

10 9 8 7 6 5 4 3 2 1

Design: Glenn Howard
Publisher: Philip Cooper
Senior Editor: Michael Brunström
Senior Designer: Isabel Eeles
Senior Production Manager: Alex Merrett

Printed in Guangdong, China TT062025